SHACKLETON

ACKNOWLEDGMENTS
To David and Sheila Mortimer for all the time spent proof-reading and Gary Armstrong and the boys for providing the inspiration when the going occasionally got tough.

THIS IS A CARLTON BOOK

First published in the UK in 1999
This paperback edition published in 2002 by
Carlton Books Limited
An imprint of the Carlton Publishing Group
20 Mortimer Street
London WIT 3JW

A CIP catalogue record for this book is available from the British Library

ISBN 1 84222 603 7

Project Editor: Camilla MacWhannell
Project art direction: Diane Spender
Designer: Andy Jones
Production: Garry Lewis
Picture Researcher: Alex Pepper

Printed and bound in Dubai

SHACKLETON

The story of Ernest Shackleton and the Antarctic Explorers

GAVIN MORTIMER

Contents

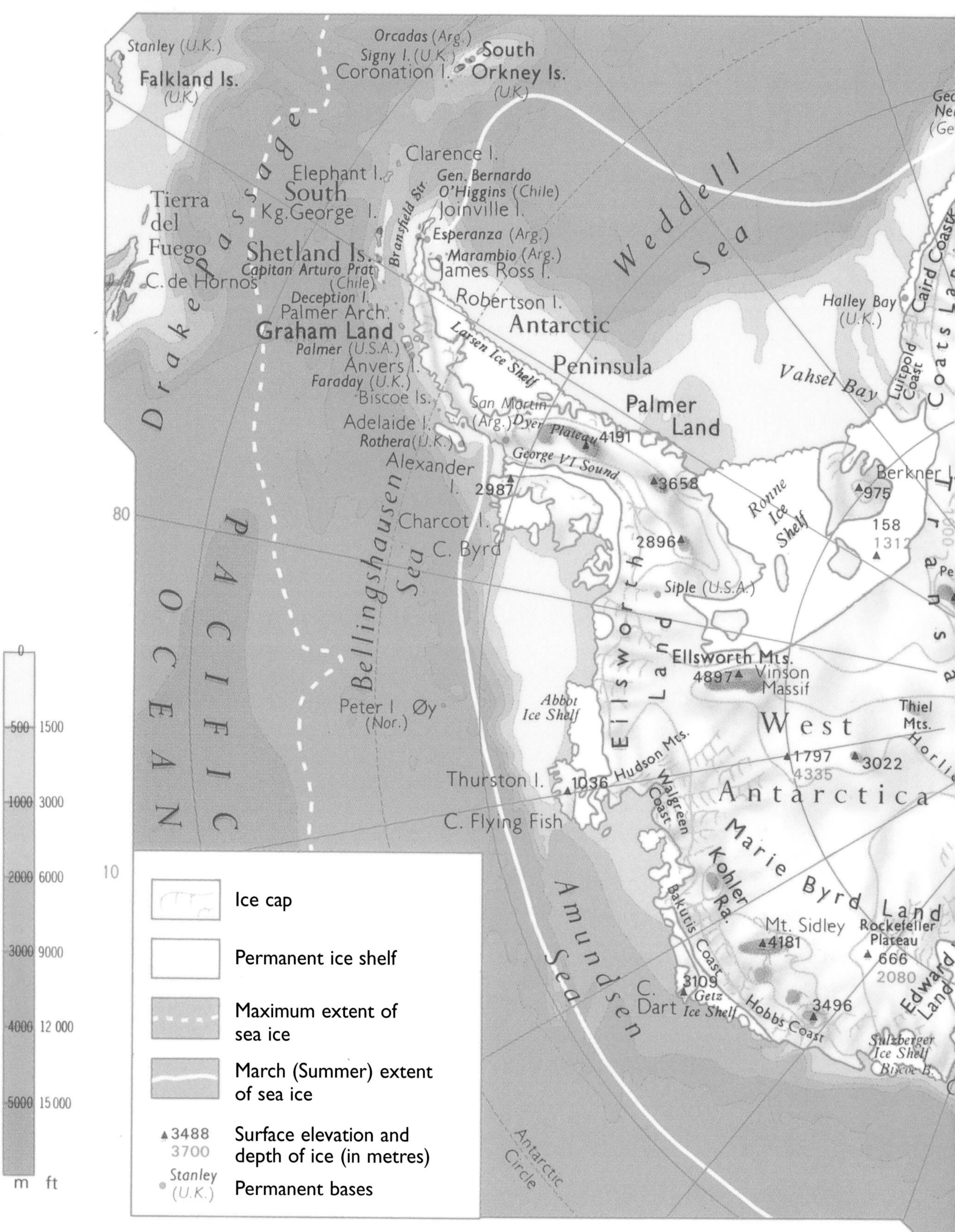
Stanley (U.K.)
Falkland Is. (U.K.)
Orcadas (Arg.)
Signy I. (U.K.)
Coronation I.
South Orkney Is. (U.K.)
Clarence I.
Elephant I.
South Shetland Is.
Kg.George I.
Gen. Bernardo O'Higgins (Chile)
Joinville I.
Esperanza (Arg.)
Marambio (Arg.)
James Ross I.
Bransfield Str.
Tierra del Fuego
C. de Hornos
Capitan Arturo Prat (Chile)
Deception I.
Drake Passage
Weddell Sea
Robertson I.
Antarctic Peninsula
Palmer Arch.
Graham Land
Palmer (U.S.A.)
Anvers I.
Faraday (U.K.)
Biscoe Is.
Adelaide I.
Rothera (U.K.)
Larsen Ice Shelf
San Martin (Arg.)
Dyer Plateau
4191
Palmer Land
George VI Sound
Alexander I.
2987
3658
Ronne Ice Shelf
Berkner I.
975
158
1312
Vahsel Bay
Halley Bay (U.K.)
Caird Coast
Luitpold Coast
Coats Land
80
PACIFIC OCEAN
Bellingshausen Sea
Charcot I.
C. Byrd
2896
Siple (U.S.A.)
Ellsworth Land
Ellsworth Mts.
4897
Vinson Massif
Peter I Øy (Nor.)
Abbot Ice Shelf
West Antarctica
Thiel Mts.
1797
4335
3022
Thurston I.
1036
Hudson Mts.
Walgreen Coast
C. Flying Fish
10
Marie Byrd Land
Kohler Ra.
Bakutis Coast
Mt. Sidley
4181
Rockefeller Plateau
666
2080
Amundsen Sea
C. Dart
3109
Getz Ice Shelf
Hobbs Coast
3496
Edward VII Land
Sulzberger Ice Shelf
Antarctic Circle
0
500
1000
2000
3000
4000
5000
1500
3000
6000
9000
12 000
15 000
m
ft
Ice cap
Permanent ice shelf
Maximum extent of sea ice
March (Summer) extent of sea ice
3488
3700
Surface elevation and depth of ice (in metres)
Stanley (U.K.)
Permanent bases
1:35 000 000

Dakshin Gangotri
(India)
Prinsesse Astrid Kyst
Prinsesse Ragnhild Kyst
Mühlig Hofmann fjell
Sør-Rondane
3630
Riiser-Larsen-halvøya
Lützow Holmbukta
Syowa (Japan)
Prins Harald Kyst
Kronprins Olav Kyst
Mizuho (Japan)
INDIAN OCEAN
60
C. Borley
Enderby Ld.
2260
Kemp Land
Stefansson B.
Mawson Coast
Mawson (Austr.)
Mac-Robertson Land
2645
C. Darnley
3355
Prince Charles Mts.
Lambert Glacier
Amery Ice Shelf
Prydz Bay
Zhongshan (China)
Davis (Austr.)
Ingrid Christensen Coast
80
American Highland
1800
Maud Land
2717
3212
3039
3318
2990
2311
1431
3556
2600
4030
1040
East Antarctica
SOUTH POLE
Amundsen-Scott (U.S.A.)
West Ice Shelf
Wilhelm II Coast
Queen Mary Land
Drygalski I.
Davis Sea
Masson I.
Shackleton Ice Shelf
3030
2570
Denman Gl.
Mill I.
100
Bowman I.
Scott Gl.
Knox Coast
Queen Maud Mts.
Beardmore Glacier
2801
3491
3488
3700
4528
Queen Alexandra Ra.
Mt. Markham
4349
2407
3087
Shackleton Inlet
Ice Shelf
Casey (Austr.)
Budd Coast
C. Poinsett
Sabrina Coast
Totten Glacier
Wilkes Land
Mt. Lister
4023
Mt. Erebus
3743
McMurdo (U.S.A.)
Scott (N.Z.)
Ross I.
McMurdo
Franklin I.
Victoria Land
Pr. Albert Mts.
Dalton Iceberg Tongue
Banzare Coast
Porpoise Bay
2216
2798
2435
4776
Ross Sea
Mt. Murchison
3502
Coulman I.
Clarie Coast
Blodgett Iceberg Tongue
Terre Adélie
Dumont d'Urville (Fr.)
George V Land
Possession I.
C. Adare
3719
Commonwealth B.
Oates Land
+Magnetic Pole 1990
70

Introduction

The South Pole is the harshest and most desolate spot on the Earth's surface. You can find it on a map at 90° South, and with the exception of a special band of explorers, that is as close as any of us will ever get to the Pole.

Bellingshausen station, named after the Russian explorer, who, in 1820, came within 20 miles of Antarctica.

Ernest Shackleton, Roald Amundsen and Captain Scott are names that will forever be linked with the South Pole. They were the men who pioneered Antarctic exploration, and they did so with clothing and equipment that would be considered laughable by modern standards.

The continent of Antarctica covers 5,000,000 square miles – one-and-a-half times the size of the USA – and represents a tenth of the world's land area. Yet less than a century ago, it was still *terra incognita*, unspoilt by mankind.

Of those millions of square miles, only a few hundred are free from a permanent covering of ice, so neither man nor beast has much affection for so barren a place. What drove men to Antarctica was the desire to explore. As Shackleton wrote to his sister, shortly after he had set foot on the continent for the very first time, "You can't think what it's like to walk over places where no man has been before."

This book chronicles the 'heroic age' of exploration in Antarctica and relates the stories of the characters who risked their lives as they sought to penetrate further south than any man before. They came from all around the world – Britain, Norway and Australia – and were soldiers, sailors, scientists and doctors. They suffered unimaginable hardships, and some remain there to this day, their bodies covered by a fresh layer of snow each year, but they were a special breed of men. As a British contemporary of Shackleton wrote, "Courage or ambition may take you to the Antarctic, but it won't take you far inside without being found out; it's courage, and unselfishness, and good temper, and helping one another, and a willingness to put in every ounce you have."

CHAPTER ONE

The *Discovery* Expedition

As the twentieth century dawned, the British were becoming increasingly alarmed that they would lose the race to the South Pole. So in 1901, an expedition sailed in the Discovery *in an attempt to grab the prize for the British Empire. In command was a 33-year-old naval officer with no previous experience of polar exploration.*

Above
Sir Clement R. Markham, President of the Royal Geographical Society, who was the driving force behind British polar exploration in the early 1900s.

The man who was prepared to trade experience for ambition when selecting a leader was Sir Clements Markham, the driving force behind much of Britain's polar exploration in the early 1900s. Born in 1830, four days after the Geographical Society (now the Royal Geographical Society) was instituted, he was elected its president in 1893 and immediately began to put into practice his plans to launch a British naval expedition to the South Pole.

Markham's obsession with polar exploration had its origins in his own brief naval career. He became a cadet in 1844, when the Royal Navy was the most powerful military force in the world. In 1850–51, he was a member of a search party dispatched to the Arctic to hunt for Sir John Franklin, the British explorer who had disappeared with his crew in 1847 while seeking the North-West Passage (their fate remained unknown until 1859, when it was discovered that all of them had died after their ship became trapped in ice).

Markham left the Navy a short while later, harbouring ambitions to become an explorer in South America. The death of his father, however, left him in a perilous financial situation, and he was forced to abandon his plans and take a succession of dull office jobs in London.

Eventually, Markham joined the India Office and, demonstrating the kind of persuasiveness that later he would use to such great effect in his role as president of the Geographical Society, convinced his bosses that the Peruvian cinchona tree, the bark of which produced quinine – a preventive treatment for malaria – should be introduced into

The sheer magnificence of a glacier in the Antarctic mountains.

India. This allowed him to travel and satisfy his wanderlust.

Markham's appointment as president of the Geographical Society coincided with a renewed interest in polar exploration. Although he was determined to beat the Norwegians and Americans to the South Pole, the Royal Navy had more pressing matters to contend with. Germany was rebuilding her armed forces, and a belligerent, menacing wind was blowing through Europe. Consequently, the Admiralty decided against funding a venture to Antarctica.

Undeterred, Markham pressed on and launched a private expedition that he hoped would capture the imagination of the British public. He soon discovered that the most difficult part of any polar trek is raising the capital, and for two years struggled to find backers. In the end, the Government provided £45,000 and saved him from embarrassment.

Now that the expedition was secure financially, Markham turned to the question of a leader, and immediately ran into problems. The organizing committee was split into two factions, and they disagreed on the type of leader required. On the one hand were Sir Clements and the Geographical Society, who felt that the venture's prime concern was geographical discovery and, therefore, demanded a naval officer. On the other was the Royal Society – disparagingly labelled "mud larkers" by Markham – who viewed the expedition first and foremost as a scientific mission and, thus, wanted a scientist to be in command.

After much argument, Markham prevailed. He had a clear picture of the sort of officer he was seeking: the successful candidate needed good manners and impeccable breeding, but most importantly had to fulfil Markham's romantic ideal of a noble and daring British adventurer.

Markham already had a man in mind, having first encountered him in 1887 as an 18-year-old midshipman during a clipper race in the West Indies. Their paths had crossed again in the intervening years, and although the young midshipman had since been promoted to lieutenant on a torpedo boat, his fierce ambition demanded a new challenge. When the officer heard about the expedition to the South Pole, he turned up on Markham's doorstep to volunteer his services. His name was Robert Falcon Scott.

Scott's early life

Robert Scott was born in Devonport on June 6, 1868, the third of six children, to John and Hannah Scott. Known to his family as "Con" – a contraction of his middle name – he could trace his ancestry to the 1745 Rebellion in Scotland, when his forebears fought alongside Bonnie Prince Charlie at Culloden.

Although there was a strong naval tradition in the family, John Scott had been considered too weak to go to sea, so instead he ran a brewery in Plymouth. Throughout his life, Robert Scott was haunted by the thought that he, too, was physically inferior to other men and, as a result, he drove himself to limits that few could match. As his biographer wrote in 1929, "All through life he was, if one may use a golfing metaphor, playing against bogey; scrutinizing his own performance to see if it could have been bettered."

As a young boy, Scott was prone to excessive day-dreaming and, displaying another of his father's

Captain Robert Scott always felt the need to prove himself physically superior to other men.

The battleship Empress of India *in 1895, one of Scott's postings that failed to enthuse him.*

shortcomings, he was considered lazy. Reproaching himself for passing his flaws to his son, Scott's father did everything he could to ensure that the boy received a good education and gained a sense of self-discipline.

After a brief spell at Foster's Naval Preparatory School, Scott became a naval cadet and joined the training ship HMS *Britannia*, on the River Dart. There, he was subjected to the harsh and repressive regime that characterized the Royal Navy at that time.

Although, by all accounts, Scott enjoyed the naval life, at times the solitary and introspective side of his nature railed against the conformity and insensitivity of the Navy, and it was around this time that he began to keep a diary. He was a gifted writer who expressed his thoughts with clarity and directness, and the legacy of this talent helped create the Scott legend that remains a century later.

After two years in the *Britannia*, Scott passed out seventh of a class of 26 and joined the *Boadicea* as a midshipman in August 1883. He spent the next four years putting his seamanship skills into practice, then entered the Royal Naval College at Greenwich, where he successfully completed his exams to become a sub-lieutenant.

Scott's first appointment as a sub-lieutenant was to the cruiser *Amphion*, stationed at Vancouver Island in Canada. On the last stage of the arduous journey to join his new ship, he caught a steamer from San Francisco to British Columbia, and sailed into the teeth of a raging gale.

Panic ensued, but the 20-year-old Scott took control of the situation, demonstrating a maturity and calmness that belied his diffident exterior. A fellow passenger recalled how, in quelling the fears of the mob, Scott "settled the quarrels and established order either by his personality, or, if necessary, by his fists". The steamer limped into port with Scott the hero of the hour.

However, he soon found the routine of a peacetime naval officer mundane, and although he was promoted to full lieutenant in 1889, he yearned for more exciting challenges. Two years later, he decided to specialize and joined a torpedo training ship, learning about a weapon that had become a favourite with the Navy. An appointment in 1896 to the battleship *Empress of India* was followed by a transfer to the *Majestic*, flagship of the Channel Squadron, but still Scott craved an escape from the humdrum existence he feared he had entered.

He recognized that he was not an exceptionally gifted officer, and the other routes to the top for ambitious, young naval officers in those days – money and family connections – were not open to him either. His younger sister Grace wrote later, "In 1899, coming home in HMS *Majestic*, he said he must look out for something to take him out of the general rut of the Navy. All this time he had been realizing that he had something to say, in some form or other as yet unknown. How could he express himself fully?"

Scott thought that the answer to the question might be found in Sir Clements Markham's National Antarctic Expedition.

Scott is elected leader

In later years, when the Scott legend had become indelibly etched in the consciousness of the British people, Markham claimed that he knew from the moment he first met him, in 1887, that this was the man fate had selected to become Britain's polar leader: "I was much struck by his intelligence, information and the charm of his manner. My experience taught me that it would be years before an expedition would be ready, and I believed that Scott was the man destined to command it."

Since then, some have questioned the veracity of Markham's words, pointing out that Albert Armitage, who was Scott's second-in-command on the *Discovery* expedition, was approached by Markham in the late 1890s with a view to his becoming the leader of the enterprise. However, the ever-ambitious Scott – either by luck or design – managed to "bump" into Sir Clements on several occasions as the plans for a venture south were coming to fruition.

In June, 1900, Scott's appointment to command the expedition was confirmed, albeit grudgingly by the Royal Society, who feared that the first Antarctic mission to leave British shores in 60 years was under the control of a man unsuited to such a role. Scott himself later admitted that, at the time, he had "no predilection for polar exploration".

With only a year until the departure date of the expedition, Scott had little time to verse himself in the myriad aspects of polar travel.

The calm before the storm: the Discovery *by the Embankment in London in 1901.*

Moving to a flat in West London, he ran to the expedition's offices in Savile Row each morning, building up his stamina for what lay ahead.

The ship Scott would command was called the *Discovery*, and it was one of the last large wooden vessels to be constructed in Britain. It was built in Dundee, the shipbuilders being instructed to make the sides 20 inches thick and reinforce the bow with steel plates. Sir Clements Markham was determined that pack ice would not prevent the *Discovery* from reaching Antarctica.

While the shipbuilders were busy in Scotland, Scott travelled to Norway in October, 1900, to seek out the oracle on all matters polar, Fridtjof Nansen, then the greatest living explorer. In 1895 Nansen had reached 86o 14'N, the furthest any man had come to discovering the North Pole.

Scott received the benefit of all of Nansen's experience, gaining a valuable insight into the skills he would need to survive a polar expedition. However, he found it difficult to stomach the most important piece of advice Nansen had to offer: it concerned the use of dogs.

Dogs would become Scott's Achilles' heel on his two expeditions south. He was a sensitive man – "to a degree which might be considered a fault", a friend and fellow explorer once said – and he was repelled by the idea of using dogs to haul supplies and equipment, then killing them for food.

Shackleton won his place on Discovery despite coming from the Merchant Navy

However, Nansen was becoming used to the British and their sentimental attitude toward dogs, which he found incomprehensible. Shortly before Scott came to see him, Nansen had met Sir Clements Markham at the International Geographical Congress in Berlin. The two men had argued about the use of dogs and polar travel. Markham insisted that men could pull more weight than dogs and that using dogs was cruel, to which Nansen replied, "I agree it is cruel to take dogs; but it is also cruel to overload a human being with work."

Despite Scott's objections to dogs, he accepted Nansen's advice and made arrangements for some to be imported from Russia in the following year.

Back in Britain, Scott turned his attention to the most important task in the planning of the expedition: choosing its members. He and Markham were determined that the Royal Navy would account for most of the crew. The latter wanted to see the glory of the expedition bestowed upon the service he still adored, while the former doubted his ability to control men from any other walk of life. For Scott to admit this publicly was a startling admission of his own weaknesses as a leader: "From a very early date I had set my mind on obtaining a naval crew. I felt sure that their sense of discipline would be an immense acquisition and I had grave doubts as to my own ability to deal with any other class of men."

Scott chooses his men

Scott was granted his wish, being given a free hand to pick his crew, most of whom came from the Royal Navy once the Admiralty had agreed to release a certain number of men. There was one glaring exception, however, an officer from the Merchant Navy called Ernest Shackleton. Over the course of the next few years, he would become Scott's bitter rival.

The root of the rivalry between the two men lay in their temperamental differences. Shackleton was an Irish-born extrovert who could recite poetry at will, Scott was the reserved English naval officer;

Shackleton had the common touch, Scott found it difficult to mix with his social inferiors; Shackleton was a born optimist, Scott was prone to bouts of depression. However, in the years leading up to the *Discovery* expedition, they had much in common. Like Scott, Shackleton was conscious of being trapped in his career.

Shortly before he heard about the National Antarctic Expedition, Shackleton had sent an angst-ridden letter to Emily Dorman, later to become his wife. "A man should strive to the uttermost of his life's set prize," he wrote. "I feel the truth of it; but how can I do enough if my uttermost falls short in my opinion of what should take the prize?"

Scott and Shackleton's second shared quality was ambition. Later, both admitted that initially their desire to explore Antarctica had not been motivated by a fascination with the region. Rather they saw the prospect as an opportunity to gain fame and fortune. For Shackleton – a man conscious of his Irish background in London society – it was also a chance to improve his social standing, particularly in the eyes of Charles Dorman, the man whose daughter he loved and wished to marry.

Shackleton secured his place on the *Discovery* through a chance encounter with Cedric Longstaff, the son of one of the expedition's most generous benefactors. A short time later, he was introduced to Cedric's father, Llewellyn Longstaff, who fell under the spell of the garrulous and charming Irishman. Longstaff was so taken by Shackleton that he asked Sir Clements Markham to find a place on the expedition for him.

Although not overjoyed at the thought of accepting an officer from a service he considered inferior, Sir Clements felt obliged at least to meet Shackleton to see for himself the qualities that had so impressed Longstaff. Once again, Shackleton's allure proved irresistible. "He is a steely, high-principled young man, full of zeal, strong and hard working," commented Markham. Shackleton was in.

Another man whose attributes included hard work and zeal was Dr Edward Wilson, whose name would become linked inextricably with Scott over the following 12 years. Wilson was the rock that Scott clung to so often in Antarctica when he felt he was drowning in a sea of depression, weighed down by the anxiety of leadership.

Born in Cheltenham in 1872, Edward Wilson was raised in an atmosphere of religious devotion that instilled in him a spiritual serenity that remained with him until his death. This air of calm, borne out of a belief that a man's destiny was pre-ordained, drew men to Wilson in times of hardship. In much the same way that soldiers turn to their padre when battle is imminent, Antarctic explorers leaned on Wilson when they felt troubled.

Scott's second-in-command, 36-year-old Albert Armitage, had been on the 1894–97 Jackson-Harmsworth expedition to the Arctic. Undoubtedly, his knowledge of polar exploration made Scott feel uncomfortable throughout the *Discovery* expedition, aware as he was of his own inexperience. Armitage, however, kept his counsel and proved his worth down south on more than one occasion.

In total, there were six officers on the expedition (including Scott), five civilian scientists – one of whom, Louis Bernacchi, had wintered on Cape Adare with Carsten Borchgrevink in 1899 – and 27 seamen, 20 of whom served in the Royal Navy. Among the seamen were three who would become fabled polar explorers: Frank Wild, William Lashly and Edgar Evans.

Wild was a small, tireless Yorkshireman who formed a friendship with Shackleton on board *Discovery* that lasted for the following 20 years.

"A MAN SHOULD STRIVE TO THE UTTERMOST OF HIS LIFE'S SET PRIZE ..."

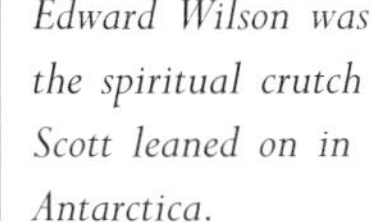

Edward Wilson was the spiritual crutch Scott leaned on in Antarctica.

Frank Wild (centre), Shackleton's right hand man, on board Endurance *in 1914.*

Scott tried to persuade Wild to journey south with him in 1910, but by then explorers usually belonged in either Shackleton's or Scott's camp, and for Wild it was the former.

Leading Stoker Lashly and Petty Officer Evans, an Englishman and Welshman respectively, were resolutely Scott's men. Both were physically strong, with stamina and courage to match. These qualities always held an appeal for Scott, and he went to great lengths to secure their services again in 1910.

The journey south

Discovery sailed from England at the beginning of August, 1901, after a brief stop at the annual yachting regatta at Cowes, which was enjoying the patronage of King Edward VII. The King came on board and addressed the crew before allowing Scott's mother to bestow upon her son the Royal Victorian Order, one of a series of new decorations that commemorated Queen Victoria, who had died in January of that year.

The death of the Queen, after a reign of 64 years, and a series of setbacks suffered by the British Army in its campaign against a supposedly disorganized Boer militia in South Africa, had left the British uncertain of their role in the new century. Thus, Scott and his men left with the unanimous backing of their countrymen. As one newspaper, the *Morning Post*, trumpeted, "Even in the throes of an exhausting struggle [the Boer War], we can yet spare the energy and the men to add to the triumphs we have already won in the peaceful but heroic field of exploration."

Discovery crossed the Antarctic Circle on January 3, 1902, and followed James Clark Ross's route along the Great Ice Barrier until, on January 29, she passed the point at which Ross had turned back and sailed into virgin waters. The very next day, the expedition made what Shackleton called "a very definite discovery" – new land that Scott named King Edward VII Land (now known as the King Edward VII Peninsula). "It is a unique sort of feeling," wrote Shackleton, "to look on lands that have never been seen by human eye before."

The SS Discovery *sails out of London in 1901 en route to Antarctica.*

At the beginning of February, the crew enjoyed a spot of light relief when a balloon, given to the expedition by the Army for carrying out aerial surveys, was launched. Scott was the first to climb into its wicker basket, followed by Shackleton, who ascended to a height of 650 feet. An unimpressed Wilson, however, declined the offer of a trip to the heavens, commenting, "If some of these experts don't come to grief over it out here, it will only be because God has pity on the foolish." To Wilson's undoubted relief, the balloon developed a puncture, making it unusable for the remainder of the expedition.

Having made the first flight in Antarctica, Scott sailed up McMurdo Sound on February 8, looking for a base from which he could launch his attempt to reach the South Pole.

Scott and his men (left) inflate the balloon that proved a short-lived success.

Scott's leadership skills

By the time *Discovery* had found a winter haven, Scott's men had begun to learn some of their leader's shortcomings. On the journey south, Wilson had noted that he was "quick-tempered and impatient", while others found themselves on the receiving end of the rough side of his tongue. His mood swings, occasional pettiness, impatience and solitary nature made it difficult for the men to form an affection for him.

"One of the boys ..."

One of Scott's greatest failings as a leader was his inability to be "one of the boys" yet command instant respect and obedience. Admittedly, only a fortunate few have this gift, but Shackleton was one of them. Scott, on the other hand, always felt uneasy when mixing with the "lower deck".

Scott further alienated himself from the seamen aboard the *Discovery* by his adherence to naval traditions, when logic and common sense called for flexibility. Able Seaman Thomas Williamson kept a diary throughout the expedition to Antarctica, and its entries include several stinging attacks on Scott: "They must seem to think we are some automobile which only wants oiling to keep it on the go, instead of human beings." On another occasion, there is almost an impression of potential mutiny as Williamson describes the disaffection with Scott: "Fancy all hands being drove

Scott hard at work in his separate quarters during the 1910-12 expedition.

on deck on a day like this just because the skipper wants to inspect the mess deck. This and a few more petty items is causing a lot of discontent on the mess deck." Yet ten years later, Williamson wept when he and the rest of the search party discovered Scott's frozen body.

Undoubtedly, Scott had many faults as a leader and a man, but those with him were intelligent, courageous and down-to-earth souls who wouldn't have followed him if they thought him an incompetent fool. They stuck with Scott because they admired and respected him, despite his flaws.

Apsley Cherry-Garrard, who was with Scott on the 1910–12 expedition to Antarctica, was well aware of his leader's shortcomings, calling him a temperamentally weak man. Yet Scott's appeal to Cherry-Garrard, and to so many others, was his awareness of his weaknesses and his absolute determination to subjugate them. "His triumphs are many," Cherry-Garrard wrote of Scott after his death. "But the Pole was not by any means the greatest of them. Surely the greatest was that by which he conquered his weaker self, and became the strong leader whom we went to follow and came to love."

The early mistakes of the *Discovery* expedition

With the expedition firmly ensconced at Hut Point on Ross Island, attention turned to the problem of polar travel. Scott and his men had arrived in Antarctica blissfully unaware of how to use skis, and although they had dogs, none of them had been trained as a dog-driver, a skill that takes months to perfect. On February 18, 1902, a race was held between two teams of dogs, the intention being to discover the most effective way of handling them.

The Discovery *stuck in the ice on Ross Island.*

One, under Louis Bernacchi, was treated with kindness and in such a manner as to please the British sense of decency. The other, commanded by Albert Armitage, and in accordance with the advice laid down by Fridtjof Nansen, felt the crack of the whip.

Bernacchi's team won, although the race was marred by confusion from the start, and doubtless Scott felt a sense of satisfaction at not having to use what he considered unnecessary force on the dogs. In reality, however, he could ill afford any sense of achievement, for if the race had demonstrated anything, it was that Scott and his men knew virtually nothing about driving dogs on ice.

They knew even less about skis, and the first attempts by the expedition to get to grips with them proved disastrous. Charles Ford, a steward, broke his leg, while Scott himself badly damaged a knee and spent several weeks laid up in the hut, his mood ever darkening as reports reached him of one calamity after another out on the ice.

The first concerned Shackleton, Wilson and Hartley Ferrar, who had set off on the first major journey of the expedition on February 19. They had headed south-east, up on to the barrier, toward White Island.

The trio had neither skis nor dogs, and when they encountered their first blizzard, hours after leaving Hut Point, they realized that Burberry cloth – the fabric used for most of their clothing – did little to keep frostbite at bay. The blizzard was still raging when they tried to pitch their tent at the end of the first day, a skill none had practised before. Wilson said later that they were "hanging on like grim death to the tent pole to prevent the whole bag of tricks going to blazes".

Wilson, Shackleton and Ferrar arrived back at Hut Point three days later, bewildered and frostbitten, but at least alive. Unfortunately, a 12-man party under the command of Lieutenant Royds, which left in early March to leave a message for their relief ship at Cape Crozier, wasn't so lucky.

It didn't take Royds long to realize that they were hopelessly under-prepared for their venture – they had only three pairs of skis between the 12 of them – so he ordered half of the party to return to Hut Point. The remainder continued toward the cape.

A rare sight in Antarctica – Captain Scott on skis!

Antarctica has a habit of making men pay for their folly in underestimating its power, and the return party was soon overtaken by a blizzard. Pitching camp on top of a peninsula, the men waited for the blizzard to blow itself out, but instead the storm hammered on their tent with increasing violence.

Unable to light their primus lamps, and with their inadequate clothing inviting frostbite, they made a fateful decision to try to march through the blizzard. They slipped and slithered over the ice in their leather boots until the inevitable happened: one of the men, Seaman Vince, lost his footing and slid 1,000 feet down a slope that led to an ice cliff and a drop into the sea. Vince's comrades could only watch in horror as he struggled in vain to prevent himself from disappearing over the cliff. His body was never recovered.

Somehow, the remaining men managed to flounder back through the blizzard to safety, and although Scott was devastated by the loss of Vince, he knew that only good fortune had prevented a far greater tragedy. "Food, clothing, everything was wrong," he admitted. "The whole system was bad."

The southern journey

Scott had little time and, more importantly, few resources with which to rectify the mistakes of the first forays on to the ice before he departed on the major objective of the expedition, the 720-mile trek to the Pole.

"THE HEEL OF THE ADVANCED FOOT NEVER PLANTED BEYOND THE TOE OF THE OTHER."

On November 2, 1902, Scott, Wilson and Shackleton, along with 19 dogs harnessed to five sledges, left their comrades to embark on their journey south. Although Scott made no specific mention of the Pole, he was determined to make it their goal. Wilson, the least obsessive of the group, was left to voice their hopes: "Our object is to get as far south in a straight line on the Barrier Ice as we can, reach the Pole if possible."

The first few days of the journey went smoothly, and the trio made steady progress. However, Scott's inexperience was being pursued relentlessly across the ice by reality, and gradually his shortcomings began to take their toll.

Once again, it was Scott's blind spots – skis and dogs – that proved most costly. Initially, the dogs pulled well and impressed the three explorers, but that was because a support party was ahead of them, laying supplies along their route. As long as the dogs had a scent to follow, they pulled for all their worth. But when the support party turned back to the ship, on November 15, the dogs began to lose interest. It was a concept that the Norwegians understood, but it had escaped Scott.

To compound the dogs' unhappiness, they were being expected to pull loads of 150 pounds each, which was far too much, and Scott was driving them on at a steady plodding pace, instead of in the short, sharp bursts of activity they preferred. Dogs that don't respect their master can be obstinate brutes, as Scott soon discovered.

However, it was not only the dogs that were being worked too hard. Scott and his two companions were man-hauling 200 pounds each over the ice, while their skis sat idly on the sledges. Wilson's description of the effort required to move over a surface that was becoming increasingly sticky and resistant captured the struggle involved: "The heel of the advanced foot never planted beyond the toe of the other."

As the dogs grew more ineffectual, the three men began relaying their supplies, carrying half the load forward for a short distance, then returning for the remainder. They continued in this fashion for 31 days, moving 109 miles nearer the Pole, but covering three times that distance as they retraced their steps time after time.

A month into their journey, it dawned on them that they weren't going to make it, nor even come close to the Pole. The deterioration of the dogs – they were further debilitated by food poisoning – meant that Scott had to cut their own rations as their progress slowed, and on December 21, Wilson found the first signs of scurvy in both Shackleton and Scott.

Shackleton, Scott and Wilson take a well-earned break on Christmas Day 1902.

Scott and Wilson pose for the camera at 82° 17'S, the furthest south man had ever been.

Wilson urged his leader to turn back, but displaying the streak of pig-headedness that would have such tragic consequences ten years later, Scott insisted on ploughing forward. "We cannot stop, we cannot go back," he said. "We must go on."

On December 30, they reached their furthest point south, 82°17'S, and Scott finally swung around to head north. Although he was 250 miles closer to the Pole than any other man had been, he was beset by anxiety. This was not because he feared for their safety on the return journey, but because they had covered fewer than 400 miles, less than half the distance to his El Dorado.

"The best of luck to all of us," were Wilson's words when the three of them started on their journey home, for he alone realized the dangers they faced. Their daily intake of 4,000 calories was not adequate, and the scurvy that he had detected in Shackleton was weakening him every day.

On January 18, with the *Discovery* still 100 miles to the north, Shackleton collapsed from his illness and became a passenger for the remainder of the trip. All the dogs having died, Scott and Wilson hauled the sledges, while Shackleton staggered alongside. Occasionally, he used skis, but like Scott, he preferred to tough it out on foot.

Scurvy – the hidden enemy

Scurvy was a common killer of sailors and explorers until comparatively recently. It is caused by a deficiency in the diet of vitamin C, the lack of fresh fruit and vegetables making those at sea or in the polar regions particularly vulnerable. In the eighteenth century, one British admiral lost 300 of his 500 men to the disease, the symptoms of which include swollen muscles, spongy gums, impaired vision, exhaustion and haemorrhaging. In 1902, medical evidence suggested that scurvy was contracted from tainted food. It wasn't until 1912 that research began to provide evidence that a lack of vitamin C was the cause. Interestingly, most animals can synthesize the vitamin for themselves, the exceptions being guinea pigs, monkeys and humans.

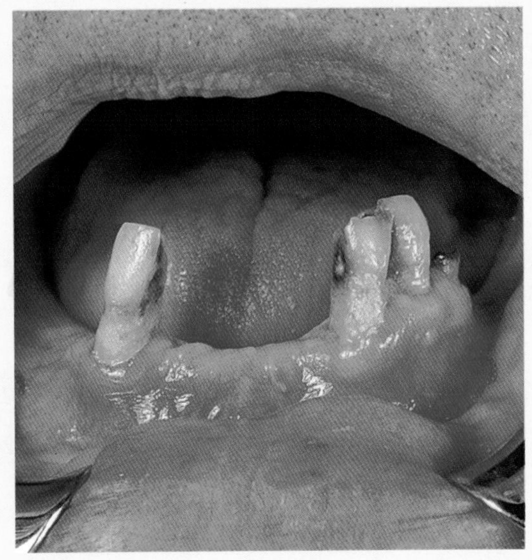

On February 3, they sighted *Discovery* after 93 days on the ice. They had covered approximately 900 miles, but all three realized how close they had come to losing their lives.

Shackleton returns home

When Scott, Shackleton and Wilson arrived at the *Discovery*, Bernacchi described them as being "almost unrecognizable". Their unkempt hair, wild beards and bloodshot eyes provided ample evidence of how Antarctica had nearly claimed them for itself.

Awaiting the three when they returned was a relief ship, the *Morning*, sent from Britain with orders for Scott to sail the *Discovery* to New Zealand. Reluctantly, he tried to prepare the ship for departure, but found the ice unwilling to release her. Struggling to contain his pleasure, he told the captain of the *Morning* that he would have to remain for another year. This additional time in the Antarctic would allow him to try to redeem his recent poor performance.

The Antarctic dining table: but Scott failed to realise how seal meat could help him.

Scott took the arrival of the *Morning* as an opportunity to rid his expedition of some of the less satisfactory members of the party. He called for eight volunteers, and got eight, nearly all from the Merchant Navy and the very men he would have chosen if he is to be believed. Although there is no evidence to suggest that he leaned on the men to return, it seems more than a coincidence that all those he wanted to depart volunteered of their own accord.

Scott also insisted that Shackleton returned because of his ill health. "He ought not to risk further hardships," he said, although already the Irishman was showing signs of rapid recovery. The swollen gums, dizziness and coughing up of blood – all classic signs of scurvy – had abated since he had gained access to fresh meat. Shackleton was devastated by Scott's order. He turned to Armitage, his fellow Merchant Navy officer, and asked him to intercede on his behalf. When Armitage approached Scott to persuade him to

Shackleton's last view of Antarctica as the Morning sails north in March 1903.

allow Shackleton to remain, Scott allegedly told his second-in-command, "If he does not go back sick, he will go back in disgrace."

Scott's desire to be rid of Shackleton should be examined in the context of the southern journey as a whole. While it hadn't been a total failure, Scott appreciated that he had made plenty of mistakes. Among the most serious of these was his wilful disregard of scurvy and its causes. Both Armitage and Shackleton had tried to convince him that fresh seal meat was the most effective way of preventing the disease, but Scott's abhorrence of killing any living creature had the perverse effect of endangering the lives of his men.

Eventually, and only after Armitage had taken advantage of his commander's absence on a short sledging trip to order seal meat to be cooked for the men, Scott realized that fresh meat alleviated the symptoms of the killer disease. Despite this knowledge, he still set off for the Pole with inadequate supplies of fresh meat. When all three succumbed to scurvy on the return journey, they could have copied the Norwegian example of eating their dogs, but Scott found the idea repugnant, even though he knew his feelings "smacked of moral cowardice", of which he was "heartily ashamed".

Shackleton's collapse, however, offered Scott a peg on which to hang the failure of the journey. He seized the opportunity of humiliating Shackleton by ordering him home as a virtual invalid, even though Wilson was taking longer to recover from the ravages of the trek.

The *Morning* slipped out of McMurdo Sound on March 2, 1903, with an inconsolable Shackleton on board. However, his despondency lifted for a brief moment when, in his own words, "the men [from the *Discovery*] came up on deck and gave me three parting cheers".

No doubt, Shackleton's agony was prolonged by memories of entertaining his fellow officers at Hut Point, prior to the start of the southern journey. In an amusing skit, he had played the heroic polar explorer fêted upon his return by the kings and queens of Europe. Aboard the *Morning*, he must have feared that he was returning bearing the stigma of a weakling.

CHAPTER TWO

Ernest Shackleton

Shackleton's early return from Antarctica was an enormous blow to a man eager to prove himself in the British Empire. Ever since he had moved from Ireland to England as a young boy, he had felt like an outsider fighting to win acceptance.

Throughout his life, Ernest Shackleton was conscious of his Irish background. Although his family hailed originally from Yorkshire, he considered himself more Irish than Anglo-Irish, and resented jibes made in London society about his origins.

Ernest's father, Henry Shackleton, like Scott's father, had been barred from military service on the grounds of infirmity. Although Shackleton never talked openly about his father in the same way that Scott did, it seems probable that, like his rival, he used his father's fragility to drive himself physically.

Unable to join the Army, Henry Shackleton moved to the rolling countryside of County Kildare, 25 miles west of Dublin, and became a farmer. He married and had ten children, the second of whom was Ernest, born on February 15, 1874. Ernest was the elder of two brothers, and he came to be idolized by his eight doting sisters. His early days were spent in relative happiness with a loving mother and a father who exercised control, but not the over zealous paternal discipline that characterized the Victorian era.

However, during the late 1870s, Shackleton's father found it increasingly difficult to provide for his large family, and in 1880 he made the bold decision to give up farming. He took his wife and children to Dublin, where he read medicine at Trinity College. Four years later, having qualified as a doctor, Henry Shackleton was on the move again, this time to England, where he settled in South London and began his medical career.

Dulwich College, where Shackleton first became aware he was an outsider.

LEFT MIDDLE Shackleton during his Dulwich days.

BOTTOM LEFT The Shackletons. Ernest is standing at the back of the group while Frank is reclining on the rug.

Ernest was sent to Dulwich College, a public school within walking distance of the family home. It was at Dulwich that Shackleton first became aware that he was an "outsider", his Irish brogue marking him as being different from the other boys. A school magazine, *The Captain*, looking back on his time at Dulwich after he had found fame, reflected that he was "rather an odd boy who, in spite of an adventurous nature and the spirit of romance that was in him, loved a book better than a bat".

None the less, Shackleton was a popular boy with a keen sense of humour, a love of practical jokes and a belligerent streak that earned him the nickname "The Fighting Shackleton". No doubt this was the result of many a playground scrap initiated by jibes about his place of birth.

Shackleton's father tried to persuade his son to follow him into the medical profession, but he had set his heart on a life at sea. He had drifted through school, bored by the routine and desperate to break free of the confines imposed upon him. In the spring of 1890, two months after turning 16, Shackleton left Dulwich and joined the Merchant Navy.

Frank Shackleton

While Shackleton was away on the high seas, his younger brother, Frank, was taking the first boisterous steps down a path that would end several years later in scandal, intrigue and disgrace.

Frank was a dandy who threw himself wholeheartedly into the beau monde of the English aristocracy in the early 1900s. A flamboyant homosexual, he was blessed with his elder brother's charm, wit and good looks, and used those virtues to gain entry into the world of lords and dukes.

One of Frank's acquaintances was Sir Arthur Vicars, Ulster King-at-Arms, who secured him a job at Dublin Castle. He divided his time between

While working at Dublin Castle Frank began his journey into infamy and disgrace.

Dublin and a luxury flat in Park Lane, London, where he began to take a keen interest in several business ventures.

Gradually, however, Frank's business interests began to gain a reputation for being somewhat dubious and unreliable, although Ernest was only too happy when his brother offered to help raise funds for his return to Antarctica in 1907. Frank's involvement with the expedition would become a major source of embarrassment for Ernest in the following years, as would the disappearance of the Irish crown jewels from Dublin Castle.

Although no one was ever convicted of stealing the jewels in June 1907, Frank was heavily implicated in the crime. Officers from Scotland Yard questioned him, but he was never charged with any offence because, it was alleged, the theft of the jewels was linked to a homosexual blackmail plot that involved several prominent members of the Establishment. If Frank Shackleton had been arrested and revealed all, it could have proved an embarrassing scandal for many well-connected people.

ERNEST STOOD BY HIS BROTHER.

Ernest stood by his brother during these turbulent times, even though he knew his reputation was being tarnished by association with his errant sibling. Finally, however, in 1913, Frank's luck ran out and he was charged with defrauding an elderly lady. He was convicted in October of that year and sentenced to 15 months' hard labour.

Although Ernest was never involved in his brother's shady business dealings – on one occasion, a man who had libelled the explorer was forced to apologize when Ernest threatened to sue him – he was deeply shamed and disowned Frank. Ernest's rejection and his own fall from grace broke the spirit of the younger Shackleton, who changed his name when he was released from prison and lived out his days as an antiques dealer on the south coast of England.

Life in the Merchant Navy

When Shackleton announced his intention to go to sea, his father explored the possibility of securing him a place on one of the Royal Navy's cadet-training ships. However, with a wife who spent most of her days ill in bed, and another nine children to support, Henry Shackleton could not afford to finance Ernest's training. Instead, he took advantage of a family connection and sent his son to Liverpool, where the boy found a berth on the rigger *Hoghton Tower*. Shackleton had little time to acquaint himself with his new ship before he found himself sailing around Cape Horn, bound for Chile.

Although Cape Horn had the reputation of being the grave of many a sailor, Shackleton seemed to enjoy his new life. He signed on for another four years, sailing regularly between England and South America, and enjoying the camaraderie that arose from shared hardships.

In 1894, he passed his second mate's exams and said goodbye to the *Hoghton Tower*. The Merchant Navy still appealed to Shackleton, but by now he was 20 years old and seeking promotion. He secured a berth on the *Monmouthshire*, and while the prospects for advancement weren't good, the position allowed him the time to study to become a first mate. He completed the exams successfully, and in 1898 became a master, qualified to take charge of any British vessel.

The Tintagel Castle *in 1900, laden with refugees fleeing from the Boer War.*

For a 24-year-old, he had reached heady heights in a short space of time. But Shackleton measured success in terms of achieving glory, and he had had little opportunity to do so in the mercantile marine. The same stirrings of ambition that had propelled Scott to badger Sir Clements Markham for command of the *Discovery* expedition, led Shackleton to seek an adventure that would mark him out as an exceptional man.

A position with the Union Castle Line in 1899 perked him up, particularly in early 1900, when his ship, the *Tintagel Castle*, carried British soldiers bound for the Boer War to southern Africa. One of the soldiers aboard his ship was the young Lieutenant Cedric Longstaff, whose father was one of the most generous backers of the *Discovery* expedition. Shackleton's friendship with Cedric led to his introduction to Sir Clements Markham and a place on the Antarctic expedition.

Shackleton the schemer

Upon his return from Antarctica, Shackleton spent most of his time aboard the *Morning* brooding on the events that had led to his early departure from the *Discovery* expedition. His pride had been severely dented by his physical collapse, and as soon as he arrived in England, in June, 1903, he began looking for a means of returning south.

Money, notably the lack of it, was Shackleton's main stumbling block. To overcome this, he resigned his Merchant Navy commission and sought a means of becoming rich quick. "My fortune is all to make, but I intend to make it quickly," he said.

attempt at paying homage to Shackleton while trying to ingratiate themselves with Scott, who was present in the audience. In reality, Shackleton had repeated many of the mistakes that Scott had made during the *Discovery* expedition of 1901–03.

One of Shackleton's most glaring errors concerned the traditional British polar explorer's blind spot – dogs. Prior to the departure of the *Nimrod*, Shackleton took time to consult Fridtjof Nansen, as all polar explorers invariably did when planning an expedition. The Norwegian told him unequivocally that he must not make the same mistake that Scott had made six years earlier by neglecting to make proper use of dogs in the Antarctic. Shackleton thanked Nansen for his time and advice, and promptly ordered a dozen Manchurian ponies for the expedition.

Shackleton considered ponies ideal for polar travel: "hardy, sure-footed and plucky," he called them, but five of the dozen he took with him on the *Nimrod* were dead a month after landing, and the others swiftly followed when he used them in his attempt to reach the Pole. Not only did he err in taking the ponies in the first place, but he also compounded this blunder by not including a skilled horseman in the expedition. (Scott took horses with him on the *Terra Nova* expedition three years later, but in Captain Oates, he had a man who was able to get the best from the animals.)

Shackleton's aversion to dogs is difficult to fathom. After his return from the *Discovery* expedition, he had spoken in glowing terms of their performance, but he had changed his mind by the time he went south again. "Some misunderstanding must lie behind the English view of the use of the Eskimo dog in the polar regions," Roald Amundsen once wrote. "Could it be that the dog has not understood his master? Or is it the master who has not understood his dog?"

Shackleton also ignored Nansen's advice to take skis with him, and it was probably this oversight that cost him the race to the Pole. "Had we taken skis on the southern journey [during 1908–09] and understood how to use them like the Norwegians, we would presumably have reached the Pole," he said during a lecture after his return. So why did he not trust skis?

For the answer to that question, it is necessary to consider Shackleton's collapse during the *Discovery* expedition. Undoubtedly, the skis had saved his life when he was too ill from the effects of scurvy to continue man-hauling, but now in his mind he associated skis with the darkest moments of his life, when he was humiliated by Scott. Shackleton seemed determined to prove that he had the strength and courage to man-haul all the

Dogs vs ponies

Dogs were a better choice for polar travel for three reasons. Firstly, they pattered across the terrain, while ponies, with their greater weight, sank deep into the snow; secondly, being carnivores, dogs could be fed on the plentiful supply of seal meat in Antarctica, but herbivorous ponies couldn't live off the land and all their food had to be brought by ship. Lastly, the thick fur of dogs was well suited to the harsh environment of the Pole, and at night they simply buried themselves in the snow. Ponies, on the other hand, had to be kept out of the wind and covered with blankets – hard work for men who had enough trouble looking after themselves.

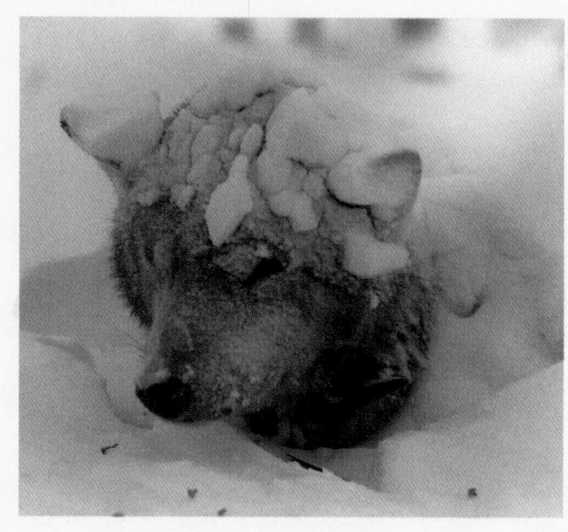

Fridtjof Nansen inspecting a seal aboard the Fram *on the 1913 expedition.*

way to the Pole. Man-hauling, after all, was considered "manly" by the British public. Shackleton feared that if he reached the South Pole on skis, his achievement wouldn't be acknowledged because he would have "cheated". Understandably, this was a notion that the Norwegians found baffling.

Amundsen, who did become the first man to reach the Pole in 1911, studied Shackleton's report of his *Nimrod* expedition to determine what could be learned from his mistakes. He was moved to conclude that "if Shackleton had been equipped in a practical manner; dogs, fur clothes and, above all, skis...and naturally understood their use, well then, the South Pole would have been a closed chapter".

But what Shackleton lacked in technical expertise, he more than made up for in what Amundsen called his "courage and willpower". As Shackleton prepared to return to Antarctica in 1907, these were two qualities that would be put to the sternest of tests during the coming two years.

CHAPTER THREE

The *Nimrod* Expedition

Ever since his collapse on the Discovery *expedition, Shackleton had yearned to return to the Antarctic to prove himself the equal of Scott. Marriage and business had tempered his enthusiasm only slightly, and by 1907 his "wanderfire" was pulling him south once more.*

Shackleton was obsessed with the Antarctic; Scott felt it his duty to venture south. That was the essential difference between the two explorers.

While Scott's expeditions were Establishment-inspired and backed by the Royal Navy, Shackleton was an independent adventurer who financed his own expeditions and had no ties to any institution. He went south because the Antarctic was in his blood and, as he had written to his sister during the early stages of the *Discovery* expedition, "You can't think what it's like to walk over places where no man has been before."

Exploration for its own sake, however, was not the sole reason for Shackleton's love affair with Antarctica. Certainly he wanted to be first at the South Pole, not only because this would ensure him a place in the history books, but also because the financial rewards would set him up for life. Before the *Nimrod* expedition had even sailed from England in 1907, he had negotiated a £10,000 deal with a publishing company for the rights to his account of the expedition if they reached the Pole. His appetite was further whetted by the prospect of a world lecture tour and the inevitable newspaper coverage it would create. In addition to satisfying his desire for fame and fortune, this would help assuage the guilt he felt at leaving his young family behind.

Emily Shackleton was the unsung heroine of her husband's polar exploits, for her patience, tolerance and loyalty were sorely tested every time he disappeared to Antarctica. Of course, when she had married him in 1904, part of his attraction had been the mystique of the "explorer", but Shackleton had made vague promises to her (as he did throughout their marriage) that he intended to settle down and be a dutiful husband.

Initially, Shackleton tried to adapt to married life, but being a dutiful husband wasn't in his nature. Although he loved his wife and adored their three children, the drudgery of domestic life stultified him. Going south was a convenient excuse for escaping from the mundane side of his marriage. "I never willingly hampered his ardent spirit or tried to chain it to the domestic life which meant so much to me," Emily wrote after her husband's death. "He used to say he went on the *Discovery* to 'get out of the ruck' for me! – it was dear of him to say it because I cannot flatter myself that it was only for me – it was his own spirit, a soul whipped on by the 'wanderfire'."

Shackleton wasn't oblivious to the hurt he caused Emily when he departed. He tried to comfort her each time with promises of "never will

The Nimrod *ploughs through the ice at the start of Shackleton's 1907 expedition.*

Emily Shackleton, with her husband, aboard Endurance *in 1914. This traumatic expedition kept them apart for three years.*

I go on this sort of thing again", but Emily knew her husband too well to believe him. "He is so suited to the work," she wrote to a friend in 1909, "that one has to put one's own feelings aside."

During the preparations for the *Nimrod* expedition, Shackleton concentrated on ensuring that everything was satisfactory, taking it for granted that Emily would look after their two children, one of whom was less than a year old. It was only when he had left England, and had time to think about his wife, that Shackleton was able to express his affection for her and unburden himself of the guilt he felt at leaving her. "I can see you just as you stand on the wharf," he wrote to Emily from the *Nimrod*. "My heart was too full to speak... If I failed to get the Pole and was within 10 miles and had to turn back it would or will not mean so much sadness as was compressed into those few minutes."

Scott stokes Shackleton's "wanderfire"

When Shackleton returned from the *Discovery* expedition, he bore Scott no grudge. The pain and humiliation he felt were mainly a result of his own physical breakdown, and although he had been reluctant to leave Antarctica, he cursed himself, not Scott, when he arrived in England.

When Scott returned in 1904, he and Shackleton spoke amicably on several occasions. In his role as secretary of the Royal Scottish Geographical Society, Shackleton arranged for his former commander to address the society in Edinburgh.

The publication of Scott's *The Voyage of the*

"Discovery", in 1905, shattered that amicable relationship. Filling two volumes, the account, according to the publishers, was based on Scott's diaries from the expedition. "A masterly work," said *The Times Literary Supplement*, but in Shackleton's opinion, the only thing masterly about it was its deceit.

Scott portrayed Shackleton as a weakling who encumbered the expedition. Entries from his original diary had been altered to exaggerate Shackleton's decline and paper over any cracks in his own leadership. The changes were subtle, but stinging. "Shackleton started in his harness but after an hour we put him on the sledge to break the speed when it tended to overrun," Scott had written in his diary on January 21, 1903. In *The Voyage of the "Discovery"*, however, the entry read, "We have had a brisk southerly breeze and, setting our sail, got along at a fine rate. For a time Shackleton was carried on the sledges." The book drove a wedge between the two men that was loosened only by death.

When Shackleton announced his intention to return south, Scott was at sea with the Atlantic Fleet. He was furious when the news reached him. Scott had been formulating a plan for his own return to the South Pole, and his first thought was that Shackleton had learned of this and launched a pre-emptive strike. Scott wrote to Wilson, who, over the course of the following few weeks, would

In happier times: Shackleton, Scott and Wilson at the start of their unsuccessful trek to the Pole in November 1902.

act as a mediator between the two quarrelsome explorers. He demanded to be told if Shackleton had known of his intentions. "I have good reason to think that he knew nothing," replied Wilson. "I myself have never heard a hint of your going south again."

Scott was not placated, his feelings of exasperation no doubt exacerbated by his distance from the heart of the controversy. Towards the end of February, he wrote to Scott Keltie, secretary of the Royal Geographical Society, saying, "Of course it may be a coincidence but it looks as though he had an inkling of my intentions and has rushed to be first in the field. It looks like this yet I cannot quite believe it of him... Shackleton owes everything to me as you know."

Piqued by what he perceived as impudence on the part of Shackleton, Scott considered the expedition an intrusion into his own territory and finished his letter to Keltie by saying, "I believe every explorer looks upon certain regions as his own... I hold it would not have been playing the game for anyone to propose an expedition to McMurdo Sound until he had ascertained that I had given up the idea of going again."

Wilson became embroiled in the increasingly hostile row between the two, and sided with Scott. "The gilt will be off the gingerbread," he wrote in a letter to Shackleton, suggesting that reaching the Pole from the base at McMurdo Sound wouldn't be sporting behaviour. This hit at Shackleton's weak spot: as far as he was concerned, the worst thing a man could do was not play the game (which was why he believed that man-hauling was preferable to using skis). Reluctantly, he agreed to abide by Scott's wishes and keep away from McMurdo Sound. "By doing so," he gloomily informed Keltie, "I much diminish any chance of success in the way of a long journey."

In April, Scott, Shackleton and Wilson met to confirm the arrangement. It was agreed that Shackleton would steer clear of McMurdo Sound

A recent shot of McMurdo Sound, the source of so much angst in 1907.

and keep to the east of 170°W. Scott was satisfied. "If as you say, you will rigidly adhere to it, I do not think our plans will clash," he told Shackleton.

The British Antarctic Expedition

When Shackleton announced his intention to go south again, in February, 1907, he had a little over seven months to prepare. Avoiding the coyness that Scott had demonstrated before and during the *Discovery* expedition, he stated his aims from the outset: "I do not intend to sacrifice the scientific utility of the expedition for a mere record-breaking journey, but say frankly, all the same, that one of my great efforts will be to reach the southern geographical Pole."

Shackleton called the venture the British Antarctic Expedition, telling his wife how proud he was to be trying for the Pole on behalf of "400 million British subjects". Not all of those subjects reciprocated his sense of pride, however, the Royal Geographical Society was noticeably lukewarm in its reaction to his announcement. As indeed was King Edward VII who, at first, refused to give the expedition his royal patronage. Later, however, during an inspection of the *Nimrod*, he presented Shackleton with the Royal Victorian Order – the same medal he had given to Scott in 1901.

The King's reluctance to give Shackleton his seal of approval had been influenced by the parlous state of the latter's financial affairs in the months leading up to the expedition. Until the moment he sailed, Shackleton was not entirely sure he had enough capital, but using all his powers of persuasion, and his not inconsiderable charm, he contrived to scrape sufficient funds together in time.

Shackleton's limited resources prevented him from purchasing the vessel he had set his heart on. Instead, he had to make do with a £5,000 sealer called *Nimrod*. She was 40 years old, small, cramped and not, to use a nautical expression, particularly shipshape. However, Shackleton had to live with the vessel's shortcomings, as time was of the essence, and he had still to finalize the members of his expedition.

King Edward VII eventually granted the Nimrod *expedition his patronage.*

Shackleton gathered his men from all walks of life; they had little in common, except that most had never met each other when they sailed south in late 1907. Crammed together aboard the *Nimrod*, they soon became uncomfortably well acquainted with one another.

Wilson turns down Shackleton

The first man Shackleton approached when he decided to launch a new expedition was Edward Wilson. The latter was working in Scotland in early 1907, researching the causes of disease in grouse. Shackleton bombarded him with a series of letters, beseeching him to come south as his second-in-command. "You are the best man in the world for it," he wrote. Wilson refused, citing his workload as the main reason.

The Nimrod *at anchor (above) and (right) Australian Douglas Mawson.*

Greatly disappointed by Wilson's decision, Shackleton turned to a Royal Naval Lieutenant called Jameson Boyd Adams. They had first met in 1906, when Shackleton observed Adams's ship, HMS *Berwick*, from the roof of his house as it sailed up the Firth of Forth. He signalled in semaphore, inviting the officer of the watch to dinner. Adams accepted, and a year later was stunned to receive another invitation from Shackleton, this time offering him a place on the *Nimrod* as his second-in-command.

All of Shackleton's expeditions were notable for the rather haphazard manner in which he chose his men. Raymond Priestly was also on the *Nimrod* and had been accepted in circumstances as strange as Adams. He had been reading geology at Bristol University when a representative of Shackleton arrived to interview another geologist for the expedition. That candidate was unsuccessful, but Priestly happened to be passing when the interviewer asked him if he'd like to go to the Antarctic. "I'd go anywhere to get out of this place," Priestly replied and, after a brief meeting with Shackleton a few days later, he was in.

Shackleton and 14 men made up the expedition's landing party. Among them was Dr Eric Marshall, chief surgeon on the *Nimrod*, whom Priestly described as "having the build and arrogance of the class rugger forward". Marshall was indeed a gifted sportsman as well as a Cambridge graduate. He soon came into conflict with an Australian geologist called Douglas Mawson. The two men developed a mutual antipathy during the following months, but as *Nimrod* battled her way through the Southern Ocean, seasickness was the main thing on their minds.

Shackleton breaks the agreement with Scott

Nimrod had sailed from Britain at the beginning of August 1907, under the command of Captain Rupert England. He had been recommended to Shackleton by William Colbeck, who had himself turned down the opportunity of skippering the ship because he was reluctant to forgo a comfortable berth in the Merchant Navy for the rigours of the Southern Ocean.

The Nimrod *sails out of Lyttelton harbour in New Zealand, on the final leg of its journey.*

Shackleton didn't join the *Nimrod* until December. He had to remain in England to tie up loose ends concerning the expedition before he could finally escape the clutches of civilization. "I shall not be really happy," he wrote to Elspeth Beardmore, whose husband was still waiting for him to repay a loan of £1,000, "until I see the last of the ship and we are out on our own on the ice."

On the first day of 1908, Shackleton and the *Nimrod* sailed out of Lyttelton harbour in New Zealand and away from the concerns of the rest of the world for two years. On January 14, the first icebergs were spotted, and nine days later they sighted the Great Ice Barrier.

The agreement with Scott still weighed heavily on Shackleton's mind as the *Nimrod* sailed eastward, away from McMurdo Sound and toward King Edward VII Land. He was searching for Barrier Inlet – the spot where he and Scott had used a balloon to survey the surrounding land during the *Discovery* expedition – and he stayed on deck all through the night, anxiously scanning the horizon for signs of it.

Shackleton had selected Barrier Inlet as a

Shackleton's winter quarters at Cape Royds at the end of the 20th century.

JOYCES
SKIING
ACADEMY
FREE

An interior view of Shackleton's hut at Cape Royds which he used in 1907.

suitable base for his landing party, not only because it was well away from Scott's "claims", but also because it was 60 miles nearer the South Pole than McMurdo Sound. The possibility of reducing the round trip to the Pole by a total of 120 miles was enticing. By the morning of January 24, however, he was becoming increasingly worried. There was no sign of the inlet, and by his calculations *Nimrod* was further south than *Discovery* had been in 1902. Four times he calculated their position before accepting that Barrier Inlet had broken away and drifted lazily out to sea. In its place was a wide bay that Shackleton named the Bay of Whales, after the many creatures that cavorted merrily in its waters.

Shackleton was rattled. He pondered landing somewhere in the Bay of Whales, but Captain England was becoming edgy, sensing his leader's rare indecision and fearing that they could become trapped in the ice. England wanted to make for McMurdo Sound. Shackleton still wavered, however, fretting at the possible consequences of breaking his promise to Scott. The deciding factor was the intervention of Frank Wild. "Shackleton was loath to return to McMurdo Sound," he wrote in his diary, "and talked seriously of wintering on the Barrier itself. I strenuously objected to this, having seen 7 miles of Barrier floating away... Shackleton reluctantly consented."

"SHACKLETON WAS LOATH TO RETURN TO MCMURDO SOUND."

Wild feared that if they established their base somewhere in the Bay of Whales, they could suffer a similar fate to Barrier Inlet and drift helplessly out to sea. Shackleton wasn't prepared to risk the lives of his men, and with a heavy heart ordered Captain England to steer a course west. He knew the implications of such an order. "I have been through a sort of hell," he wrote to his wife, "and I cannot even now realize that I am on the way back to McMurdo Sound... I never knew what it was to make such a decision as the one I was forced to make last night."

It wasn't until the *Nimrod* returned to New Zealand, in March, that Scott heard of Shackleton's violation of their agreement. He became incandescent with rage, accusing his rival of a "breach of faith". Scott told his fiancée that "he seems to have almost deliberately adopted the part of plausible rogue and to have thrown scruples to the wind."

Mount Erebus and the South Magnetic Pole

Shackleton sailed into McMurdo Sound on January 29, 1908, with the intention of establishing his base at the old *Discovery* hut. But 16 miles of ice blocked his ship's path, forcing the expedition 20 miles north to Cape Royds on Ross Island. That put them 20 miles further from the Pole, and Shackleton cursed his misfortune: "It really seemed as though the fates were against us."

The landing party unloaded their equipment from the *Nimrod* and began constructing a hut as the ship turned northwards, away from the Antarctic and back towards civilization. For the next year, the only permanent home Shackleton's party would enjoy would be a hut measuring 33 feet by 19 feet.

With the hut erected, Shackleton contemplated the expedition's immediate future. Originally, he had intended to embark on a depot-laying journey throughout March, but they had barely established their base on Cape Royds when the ice along the shore that linked them to the Barrier broke away, leaving them stranded. They would have to wait until McMurdo Sound froze over again before they could travel south. Inactivity frightened Shackleton, so he decided that before the sun disappeared (as it does in Antarctica between the end of April and the end of August), they would make the first ascent of the 13,400-foot Mount Erebus.

For well-equipped climbers, Erebus would not have posed too much of a challenge. Apsley Cherry-Garrard, who was with Scott during his 1910–13 expedition, called it "the most restful mountain in the world...whoever made Erebus knew all about the charm of horizontal lines". However, the six men who set off to conquer the

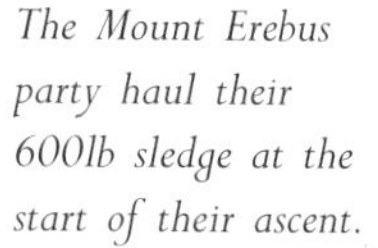

The Mount Erebus party haul their 600lb sledge at the start of their ascent.

peak at the beginning of March had none of the correct equipment. They improvised crampons by driving nails through pieces of leather and strapping them to their ski boots, but the boots were made of cowhide and provided little grip.

The climbing party, led by 50-year-old Edgeworth David, reached the summit after a five-day slog. Along the way, they had contrived to make things as difficult as they possibly could. They hauled a 600-pound sledge nearly 6,000 feet up the mountain, before continuing without it for the rest of the way, and they bivouacked because the tent had been left behind. Small wonder that the Chief Officer of the *Nimrod*, John King Davies, later said of the men who went south in 1907, "few have done so more uncomfortably or with greater hardship".

The remainder of the winter passed uneventfully, save for the occasion when Shackleton threatened to shoot the second surgeon for attacking the cook. Upon the return of the sun, David, Douglas Mawson and Alistair Forbes Mackay began a journey in search of the South Magnetic Pole.

Their quest began with a laborious trek along the coastline of South Victoria Land, the three explorers living off meat from the large numbers of seals they encountered. They crossed the Drygalski Glacier and turned inland, up on to the polar plateau. By the beginning of 1909, they had reached an altitude of 6,000 feet and were succumbing to the harsh conditions. A ferocious wind had whipped the skin from Mawson's lips, and his mouth was an agonizing mass of congealed blood. The Australian and his two companions were nearing the limits of their endurance by the time they reached their objective on January 16.

"I hereby take possession of this area now containing the Magnetic Pole for the British Empire," said David, as he planted the Union Flag at 72°25'S and 155°16'E. As the three men basked in their accomplishment, doubtless their thoughts wandered

Mackay, David and Mawson plant the Union Flag at the South Magnetic Pole.

800 miles to the south, where they knew Shackleton was battling to reach the South Pole. They had claimed the second of Antarctica's major prizes, but could their leader snatch the biggest of all?

Shackleton's attempt on the Pole

On November 3, 1908, Shackleton and three companions – Frank Wild, Eric Marshall and Jameson Boyd Adams – prepared to depart for the South Pole. As they made last-minute adjustments to the four pony-drawn sledges, each loaded with 600 pounds of supplies, they looked out across the ice. The Pole lay 747 miles to the south. "War in the old days made men," Shackleton had written as he waited for the *Nimrod* to sail from England. "We have not these same stirring times to live in and must look for other outlets for our energy and for the restless spirit that fame alone can satisfy." He had chosen the most formidable of outlets in which to test his "restless spirit".

The four men had food for 91 days, as well as the meat they would take from the ponies as they shot them along the way. This meant that they would have to average 16 miles a day. Shackleton remembered, only too well, that he, Scott and Wilson had managed an average of only six miles a day in 1902.

Shackleton and his men were forced to relay supplies because of poor conditions.

Progress was slow from the moment they left Cape Royds, and after nine days they had covered only 54 miles. That night, Shackleton burned the midnight oil, calculating how they could stretch their food even further. The outcome was a drop in rations that would allow them to extend the expedition from a maximum of 91 days to 110.

Throughout November, they plodded on, the ponies floundering through the snow, the men fighting ever-present hunger. Their unvarying diet consisted of pemmican, biscuits, cocoa, cheese, oats and sugar – 4,300 calories a day. It wasn't enough.

The first three weeks had been heavy going for all four explorers, but the cloud that had settled over them lifted on November 26, when they broke Scott's record of 82°17'S. "We have passed the Furthest South yet reached by man," a jubilant Shackleton recorded in his diary. "We are in Latitude 82°18½'S." The shadow of Scott, which had followed Shackleton for the last six years, began to fade.

The new record boosted Shackleton's confidence, and he began to wax lyrical about his surroundings. "It was as though we were truly at the world's end and we were bursting in on the birthplace of the clouds," he wrote. It was left to the Wild to add a touch of pragmatism to their progress. "I am beginning to think we shall get to the Pole alright," he confided to his diary, "but am doubtful about getting back again."

Wild's pessimism was attributable to their lack of food. By the beginning of December, the last of the four ponies, Socks, had disappeared into a crevasse, taking with her a valuable source of nutrition. By now, the men were reduced to only 3,000 calories each per day, and they had the added burden of man-hauling 1000 pounds of supplies up the 110-mile, 9,820-foot-high Beardmore Glacier, where, as Shackleton noted, "many times a slip meant death".

Christmas Day was celebrated in characteristically eccentric British fashion – with

Pemmican

The Cree Indians, of Manitoba in Canada, introduced pemmican to the world. "Pemmican" is their word for a concentrated meal consisting of lean meat that is dried in the sun, then pounded or shredded and mixed into a paste with melted fat. It proved attractive to polar explorers because it provided concentrations of both fat and protein, and could be chewed like a tough biscuit or turned into a stew (called "hoosh" by British explorers). Provided it is kept dry, it will also keep for months on end. Explorers attempted to make pemmican more palatable by adding peas and oatmeal, and when Roald Amundsen won the race to the South Pole in 1911, he fed his dogs a special canine version containing fish meal and more fat. The introduction of dehydrated foods marked the decline of pemmican as a food for explorers.

• Sledging ration: 1 man, 1 day. Cocoa, pemmican, sugar, biscuits, butter and tea

plum pudding, brandy and a dash of crême de menthe – then each puffed on a cigar as they discussed their situation. They had covered 550 miles, but still had 200 to go. In their hearts, they knew it would be suicide to continue all the way to their target, but they decided to dump all spare clothing and equipment, and try to get as near as they possibly could to the Pole.

Calling upon their last reserves of courage and stamina, Shackleton and his men advanced 65½ miles nearer the Pole during the first six days of January. On the night of the sixth, they depoted everything and prepared to make a final dash south before turning back. A blizzard taunted them for the next two days, however, confining them to their tent until the morning of the ninth, when the four emaciated figures stumbled through the snow for five hours. Then they planted the Union Jack, shook one another's hand and had their photos taken. They had reached 88°23'S, only 97 miles from the Pole. Shackleton must have been sorely tempted to go on, but as he wrote to his wife, "Better a live donkey than a dead lion."

So near yet so far: Shackleton and his men pose just 97 miles from the Pole.

Race against time

Few words were spoken by the four men as they turned north and started on the return journey. Exhaustion and hunger gnawed at them, but so did the realization that there were over 700 miles between them and safety.

Depots of horse meat had been laid along the way, but these were too far apart and inadequately marked. The four had only their own sledge tracks to guide them to the depots, and a cruel blizzard could wipe away those tracks in a few hours. Increasing their apprehension was the fact that they had lost the sledgemeter – their only means of accurate navigation – so they had to rely on guesswork and memory. As Shackleton wrote in his diary, there would be "little in the locker" when it came to a race between life and death.

They began strongly with a series of steady marches that made full use of the wind at their backs: 25 miles one day, 29 the next. Once they covered 26 miles on two cups of tea, a pot of hoosh (pemmican stew), two spoonfuls of cheese and three biscuits. However, they were weakening almost daily. "I don't know how Shackleton stands it," wrote Wild, "both his heels are split in four or five places, his legs are bruised and chafed and today he had a violent headache."

On January 20, they began the tortuous descent of the Beardmore Glacier, and all four fell into crevasses in their rush to escape the rarefied air, which was so debilitating. The next day, Shackleton collapsed from exhaustion after complaining of a headache that felt as if "the nerves were being twisted up with a corkscrew and then pulled out".

Shortly after, Adams fell asleep in his harness, and even the hitherto indefatigable Wild succumbed to the cold and hunger when within sight of the next depot. Marshall left his three colleagues in the tent to fetch supplies from the depot. It was the first solid food they had enjoyed in over 36 hours. "The hardest and most trying days we have ever spent in our lives," wrote Shackleton. A few days later, he became too weak to continue keeping his diary.

Now known as the Shackleton mountains, these peaks blocked his way in 1908.

All four were suffering from dysentery as a result of eating infected pony meat, but on February 15, Shackleton celebrated his thirty-fifth birthday with a cigar constructed from lavatory paper and pipe tobacco. It was all his men could spare. Wild recorded in his diary, "We get now less than 1½ cups of meat a day, six biscuits... three spoonfuls of pemmican; a spoonful of sugar in our tea and cocoa. How is that for more than 50° of frost and a heavy sledge at 14 miles a day and underfed?"

A week later, they saw the first sign that their hell could soon come to an end: the tracks of a depot-laying party. One of the men waiting at Hut Point had come south a fortnight earlier to lay an assortment of supplies for the four explorers at what was known as the Bluff Depot. He brought with him a team of dogs, and they had raced over the ice in next to no time. The irony cannot have escaped Shackleton.

By now, they were within 50 miles of Hut Point, but fate played her last cruel card on February 25. Marshall, who had trudged ceaselessly forward since leaving the Pole, was struck down with chronic diarrhoea. He shrugged off the attentions of his companions, however, and marched ahead, his eyes fixed on the horizon. Two days later, he was incapable of going any further.

It had been 120 days since the four explorers had set out from Cape Royds. All were ravaged by frostbite, sickness and exhaustion, yet Shackleton and Wild summoned up the willpower to march the remaining 33 miles to fetch help for Marshall and Adams, who had also become too weak to continue. Wild remembered the last few miles as a "ghastly struggle", but they made it, and by the beginning of March all four were on the *Nimrod*, recovering from their ordeal.

Shackleton the heroic explorer

Shackleton arrived back in England on June 14, 1909. He had left a little under two years earlier, under the burden of financial pressures, but he returned a hero with the entire British Empire acclaiming his outstanding feat. One newspaper wrote on the day after his arrival, "It is pleasant to think that in spite of the moanings we hear from

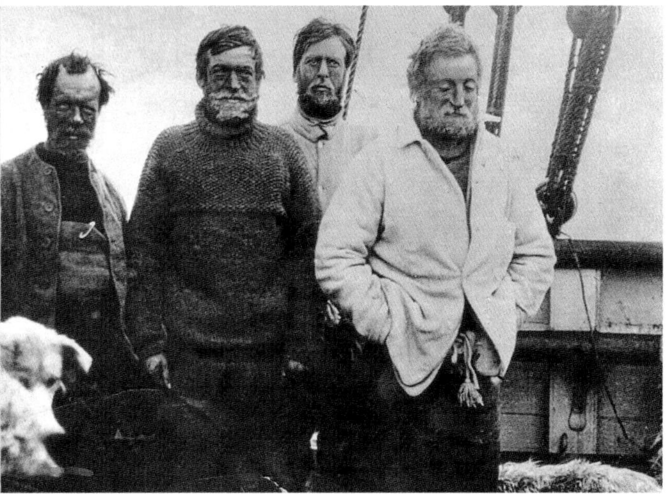

Wild, Shackleton, Marshall and Adams show the strain after their narrow escape.

time to time on the decay of British manliness, our people are still as swift as ever to idolize the Man of Action." The crowds that waited outside Charing Cross station, in central London, to cheer Shackleton did so not only out of admiration for what he had achieved in Antarctica, but also because he had reasserted the perceived British traits of courage and fortitude at a time when British self-confidence was being undermined by increasing social unrest at home, and by the threat from Germany abroad.

One of the first to greet Shackleton from the train was Scott; it hadn't been an easy gesture for him to make. Hugh Robert Mill, a member of the *Discovery* expedition, who had visited the offices of the Royal Geographical Society on the morning of Shackleton's arrival in London, recalled seeing Scott "gloomily discussing with Keltie whether he ought to go and meet Shackleton or not. He did not wish to go, but Scott was always a slave to duty."

It took courage for Scott to swallow his pride and congratulate his bitter rival. He was still seething at the broken promise, but admitted to a friend, "The private feelings incurred by past incidents cannot offset my judgement of his work. That excites my interest and admiration to an extent which can scarcely be felt by those who have no experience of polar difficulties."

Shackleton, however, was too busy milking the acclaim to pay much attention to Scott. "I never saw anyone enjoy success with such gusto," said Mills. "His whole life was to him a romantic poem, hardening with stoical endurance in adversity, rising to rhapsody when he found his place in the sun."

Shackleton had every right to enjoy his "place in the sun". The expedition had been an outstanding success, in terms of both exploration and science. They had discovered the South Magnetic Pole, the Beardmore Glacier – which would prove the route to the polar plateau – and 500 miles of mountain ranges surrounding the Great Ice Barrier.

But it was the only failure of the expedition – the unsuccessful attempt on the Pole – that won them the hearts of the Empire. The British love a glorious failure, and Shackleton's was nothing if not glorious. It contained the classic ingredients of a heroic struggle against the odds: unimaginable suffering endured with great pluck and stoicism. Shackleton was fêted wherever he went. He was knighted by Edward VII, wrote a book entitled *The Heart of the Antarctic*, received the Gold Medal of the RGS, and was guest of honour at a dinner attended by the Prince of Wales and 8,000 guests. Shackleton had arrived!

Shackleton is greeted by his wife on his return to England in June 1909.

The explorer also embarked on a lecture tour, one of his first ports of call being Norway, where his achievements were warmly applauded. He gave a talk to the National Geographical Society in Oslo, and one of the men in the audience was Roald Amundsen. He hung on Shackleton's every word, transfixed by the story of survival against the odds. It was, said Amundsen, "a wonderful achievement. The English nation has by the deed of Shackleton won a victory in Antarctic Exploration."

But Amundsen wasn't there purely to pay tribute to the Irishman; he wanted to learn from the mistakes Shackleton admitted he had made. For the Norwegian was secretly hatching a plan of his own, and its purpose was simple – to win the race to the South Pole.

Shackleton's dramatic attempt to reach the Pole made headline news.

Amundsen (front row, far left) with the crew of the Fram *in 1910.*

in 1897, when he sailed as first mate on the *Belgica*, under the command of Adrien de Gerlache.

The *Belgica* became trapped by ice in the Bellingshausen Sea in March, 1898. Thus, Amundsen and the remainder of the crew became the first men to winter in Antarctica. It wasn't a happy experience, however, although in typical fashion, he turned misfortune to his advantage by studying their predicament and what could be done to alleviate the suffering.

Four years later, Amundsen commanded his first expedition. He and six men left Norway in 1903, aboard the *Gjoa*, with the intention of being the first to sail through the North-West Passage. Since the beginning of the sixteenth century, explorers had tried to fight their way through the passage that links the Atlantic Ocean to the Pacific, but the maze of treacherous ice-filled channels defeated them all and claimed the lives of many.

For the first two winters, Amundsen and his companions lived among the Eskimos of King William Land, studying their way of life and how they had adapted to their conditions over the years. During this period, Amundsen also made several journeys to relocate the North Magnetic Pole, and learned another vital aspect of polar travel: the effectiveness of dogs. It was a lesson he wouldn't forget.

In August, 1905, the *Gjoa* slipped her moorings and sailed westward from King William Land, through the Simpson Strait. She negotiated the Dease Strait, then the Dolphin and Union Straits until, on August 26, the expedition completed the North-West Passage. Amundsen didn't return to Norway until the following year, but when he did he was given a rapturous welcome. Acclaim was a hat that fitted Amundsen well and, as he basked in the adulation of his compatriots, he was already looking for new

Amundsen (right) was for the most part a self-taught polar explorer.

Amundsen photographed standing next to Eskimo children ca. 1920.

challenges: "Having achieved the first ambition of my life," he recorded, "I began looking about for new worlds to conquer."

The race begins

The new world Amundsen had in mind was the North Pole, and he turned to Nansen for help in attaining this goal. Nansen loaned his protégé the *Fram* and also used his considerable influence to encourage backers to support Amundsen.

The plan was to leave Norway in early 1910, sail around Cape Horn and up the west coast of North America, before negotiating the Bering Strait and drifting over the North Pole. It was an audacious plan, but one that would never get off the ground. In September, 1909, Amundsen learned that the American Robert Peary had beaten him to the Pole. It was a bitter blow, which left him in a perilous predicament: "If I was to maintain my prestige as an explorer I had to win a sensational victory of some sort. I resolved upon a coup."

That coup was the South Pole, but there was a problem in going south – Scott. He had announced his plan to return to Antarctica in the same month that Amundsen had learned of Peary's triumph.

Scott had the support of many powerful figures in the British Establishment. Norway was still a fledgling nation (having gained independence from Sweden in 1905), which would not have wished to antagonize Great Britain by muscling in on territory it considered its own. Amundsen told no one of his intentions, fearful that if he disclosed his plan, the British would create such a fuss that his backers would pull out. Surreptitiously, he began to gather the supplies and equipment he needed for an attempt on the South Pole.

Amundsen was loaned the Fram *(above) from compatriot Fridtjof Nansen.*

American Robert Peary knew the value of dogs when it came to polar travel.

Amundsen didn't enjoy being deceptive, and it caused him much difficulty. He had to recruit men who thought they would be going to the Arctic, but actually were being selected for skills that would be invaluable in the Antarctic. Newspapers quizzed him on why he was still going north, when the Pole had been won by the USA; on one occasion, he even had to leave home for a few hours when he heard that Scott was on his way to ask advice about polar travel. Amundsen didn't consider that there was anything wrong in not disclosing his plans, but he wouldn't lie to Scott's face.

In August, 1910, the *Fram* left Norway and headed for Madeira, the last port of call before the voyage around Cape Horn. Or at least that was what the crew thought. They arrived in September and spent three days making last-minute preparations before the final leg of the journey to the North Pole.

On the evening of the ninth, Amundsen assembled the men on deck. "There are many things which you have regarded with mistrustful or astonished eyes," he said as he unfurled a map of Antarctica. "It is my intention to sail southwards, land a party on the Southern Continent and try and reach the South Pole."

Amundsen told them that he would understand if any of them wanted to leave the expedition. He offered a free passage home for any man who wished to return to Norway. Anxiously, he scanned their faces, looking for some reaction, and knowing full well that if the men resented the deception and refused to go along with his strategy, his reputation would never recover.

The men stood wide-eyed in disbelief as their leader's words sunk in. Although they had suspected some sort of change in plan, none had expected such a brazen ploy. Amundsen took the roll call, asking each man if he was willing to go on. "Yes" was the only answer he received. The race to the Pole had begun.

The *Terra Nova* expedition

Scott announced the British Antarctic Expedition in September, 1909 and was immediately faced with a problem that hadn't troubled the Royal Navy-backed *Discovery* expedition. The *Terra Nova* expedition would have to rely on public support for the necessary £40,000 because the Admiralty refused to fund another trip south. The thought of traipsing around the country, with cap in hand, didn't fill Scott with much enthusiasm.

Shackleton may have loved touring the length and breadth of the land, making patriotic speeches and whipping the audience into such a frenzy that they happily parted with their hard-earned cash, but Scott's introverted and conservative nature railed at such a prospect. However, since he had failed to secure a wealthy backer in the mould of Shackleton's William Beardmore, he was left with little choice. Therefore, he embarked on a series of fund-raising events in early 1910, and slowly the money began to arrive at the expedition's offices in London.

If there was a shortage of backers willing to put money behind Scott, there was no lack of volunteers eager to join him on the *Terra Nova*.

Teddy Evans was at the forefront of raising funds for the expedition south.

Captain Lawrence Oates – as courageous an explorer as he was a cavalry officer.

Over 8,000 men offered their services, and it was Scott's second-in-command, Lieutenant Teddy Evans, who was given the task of picking the right men for the job.

Evans's exuberant and forceful personality also proved invaluable in raising funds, and Scott thought that he had found the ideal deputy. However, tensions began to rise between the two when the *Terra Nova* left New Zealand, and their relationship deteriorated steadily during the following two years, until they barely bothered to conceal their dislike for each other.

The *Terra Nova* expedition comprised a total of 33 men, drawn from all walks of life and with varying aspirations. One of those who volunteered his services did so because he was fed up with his life as a cavalry officer in India. That officer's name was Captain Oates, or "Titus" to his friends.

Oates was the quintessential upper-class English gentleman of the Edwardian era. He had been educated at Eton before joining the Inniskilling Dragoons in time to see action in the Boer War. He left South Africa with the nickname "Never-say-die" and an enemy bullet in his left thigh.

After the war, Oates had been posted to India, where he indulged his two passions in life: horses and hunting. By 1910, he had become bored with the humdrum existence of a peacetime officer and sought something more exciting. To this end, he offered himself to Scott, and it was his knowledge of horses – plus £1,000 for the expedition fund – that secured him his place.

Also from India was a sub-lieutenant in the Royal Indian Marine called Henry Bowers. Nicknamed "Birdie" on account of his large nose, Bowers was as naïve and uncomplicated as Oates was laconic and cynical. "To those accustomed to judge men by the standards of their fashionable and corseted drawing rooms Bowers appeared crude," wrote Apsley Cherry-Garrard, one of his companions in 1910. "Such men may be at a discount in conventional life; but give me a snowy ice-floe waving about on the top of a black swell...and I will lie down and cry for Bowers to come and lead me to food and safety."

Cherry-Garrard's place on the expedition owed much to Edward Wilson, who had given Scott a favourable account of the 24-year-old. A short-sighted Oxford graduate who had read classics and modern history, he appeared to offer little of practical use to Scott. However, he was taken on as assistant zoologist, and before they had even arrived in Antarctica, Scott was describing him in a letter to a friend as being "always to the front when the toughest jobs are on hand".

The depot-laying journey

The *Terra Nova* sailed into McMurdo Sound on January 4, 1911, landing the expedition at Cape Evans (named in honour of their second-in-command). Cape Evans was south of Shackleton's quarters during the *Nimrod* expedition, but 20 miles further north of where Scott had wintered in 1902–04. Two weeks after landing, the 50- by 25-foot hut was habitable and the men were enjoying the benefits of its quilted seaweed insulation.

Even though the expedition was a private venture, Scott insisted on maintaining naval traditions. Thus, the officers' and men's quarters were partitioned off with crates and boxes. Scott lived in a separate cubicle, referred to by the rest of the expedition as the "Holy of holies". There, he busied himself in writing letters home and working out the details of their attempt on the Pole.

Scott planned to leave for the Pole at the end of 1911, when the Antarctic

(Overleaf) Scott's 1911 winter quarters with Mount Erebus in the distance.

Only 5ft 4in in height, but 'Birdie' Bowers was as strong as an ox.

Oates with some of the horses he called 'crocks' after their first meeting.

summer returned. Before then, however, he had to embark on a depot-laying journey across the Barrier. He wanted to leave a ton of supplies, such as paraffin, sledging rations and food for the dogs, at 80ºS in preparation for their march.

On January 24, 13 men left Cape Evans with eight ponies and 26 dogs. They struggled across the ice, averaging only 12 miles a day, and soon were held up for three days by a fierce blizzard. It became apparent to Scott that the horses were suffering from the adverse conditions. "It is pathetic to see the ponies floundering in the soft patches [of snow]," he wrote in his diary.

Oates was responsible for the horses, but at no stage prior to the expedition's departure had he been involved with their procurement. When he had first seen them, he was not impressed. "The greatest lot of crocks I have ever seen," was his terse evaluation.

On February 13, Scott decided to send three of the weakest horses back to Cape Evans. Oates protested, saying that there would be little chance of them surviving the march back to the hut and that they should continue until they dropped. Scott ignored Oates and ordered the horses to be taken back. After only 30 miles of the return journey, two of them were dead.

Four days later, Scott called a halt at latitude

79°28'S and told the men that this was where they would establish One Ton Depot. They were still some 30 miles short of 80°S, where Scott had originally intended to construct the depot. Oates stared at Scott with incredulity. Surely, he argued, it would be wiser to drive the horses as far south as possible, before killing them and depoting their meat. Scott turned on the dissenting soldier, snapping, "I have had more than enough of this cruelty to animals and I am not going to defy my feelings for the sake of a few days' march." The Oates shook his head. "I'm afraid you'll regret it, sir," he replied.

Amundsen in Antarctica

When Scott arrived in Melbourne, *en route* to New Zealand in October, 1910, a telegram awaited him. Its contents were brief: "Am going South, Amundsen." Now Scott realized he had a race on his hands, but he knew precious little about the plans of his rival. Where did Amundsen intend to land? How many men did he have? What were his precise objectives?

Amundsen and eight men landed at the Bay of Whales on January 15, 1911. He had chosen the spot after much consideration. Shackleton had rejected the bay as a possible base three years earlier, because he feared that it wasn't permanent land and could float out to sea at any moment. Amundsen, however, had studied all the available literature on the bay and had decided that it was safe to winter there. The spot was also 60 miles closer to the Pole than Scott's base in McMurdo Sound, and this was, after all, a race.

A month after landing, Amundsen and three men, together with 18 dogs, set out on their first depot-laying journey. Four hundred miles to the west, Scott and the horses were struggling through the snow, but the Norwegians fairly skimmed across the terrain. "The dogs pull magnificently," he wrote a day after leaving his base. "Cannot understand what the English mean when they say that dogs cannot be used here."

In four days, they reached 80°S and established the depot. They had averaged nearly 20 miles a day, twice the speed of Scott's party. Amundsen allowed his men a short rest before embarking on a second depot journey. Once again, they made rapid progress early on, but then encountered tougher conditions and, although Amundsen had hoped to deposit the supplies at 83°S, he contented himself with laying his furthest depot at 82°S. This was still less than 500 miles from the South Pole and, although Amundsen didn't know it, was also more than 150 miles further south than Scott's One Ton Depot.

Amundsen had left nothing to chance in his bid to reach the Pole, but perversely it was his unbridled enthusiasm that nearly wrecked his chances. Hardly had the sun returned to warm their bodies, before Amundsen was anxious to leave for the Pole. The first date he set was August 24, but the dogs were too cold to pull properly.

Amundsen soon discovered that dogs and Antarctica were made for each other.

Scott, Edgar Evans and Bowers set out on a trial sledging journey in September 1911.

Frustrated at this delay, he paced around the base for a further two weeks until he and seven companions headed south on September 8.

They struggled across the ice for six days, before Amundsen was forced to accept that they could not continue to endure the low temperatures. Turning for home, he hitched a lift on the fastest sledge and left the remainder of the party to fend for themselves. They returned to the hut in dribs and drabs, the life of Kristian Prestrud being saved only by the loyalty of Hjalmar Johansen, who went in search of his ailing comrade. Johansen was justifiably furious with Amundsen for deserting his men, and the two had a blazing row. Amundsen

didn't like having his leadership challenged – even when he was in the wrong – and he vowed to exact revenge on Johansen. When Amundsen informed the men that they would try again for the Pole on October 19, he announced that he would take only four men with him. Prestrud and Johansen had been deserted by Amundsen once more.

Scott sets out

While Amundsen was fretting about the delay to his journey south, Scott was calmly preparing his own departure. He was phlegmatic about the Norwegian's about-face and probably realized that the race was as good as lost. Nevertheless, he was determined that they should "go forward" and do

their best "for the honour of the country without fear or panic".

Scott outlined his plan to the rest of the expedition in September, and there were no great surprises in what he had to say. Ten men would set out from Hut Point on November 1, being closely followed by a two-man dog party. Preceding all of them would be two motorized sledges, under the command of Lieutenant Evans, who, with three men, would deposit provisions on the Barrier between Hut Point and the Beardmore Glacier.

When they reached the foot of the glacier, Scott and his companions would have covered a quarter of the 1,600 miles from Hut Point to the Pole and back. It was at this stage of the journey that Scott proposed to send the dogs home, shoot the ponies, depositing the meat for food upon their return, and begin man-hauling. The plan was not open to discussion, even though the more realistic of the men must have appreciated that they were going out of their way to make life difficult for themselves. Oates was one of the few to make his thoughts known. In a letter to his mother, he wrote, "From what I see I think it would not be difficult to get to the Pole provided you have proper transport but with the rubbish we have it will be jolly difficult."

The wonders of technology were lost on the men responsible for the motor sledges.

Oates may have been a pessimist, but he was an astute pessimist: sure enough, both motor sledges broke down within 50 miles of Hut Point.

On November 21, Scott caught up with Evans and the rest of his party, who had continued on foot after the fiasco with their motorized sledges. They rested and reflected on the first three weeks of the trek south. They had covered 192 miles, but the horses were deteriorating rapidly. Three days later, Oates shot the first of them, and it soon became a difficult struggle to force the remainder to keep going.

By now, they were approaching the Beardmore Glacier, but on December 5 an unseasonally savage blizzard forced them to seek the refuge of their tents for four days. "A hopeless feeling descends on one and it is hard to fight off," wrote Scott as he

Some of Scott's party begin the exhausting task of dragging an 800lb sledge up the Beardmore Glacier.

sat helplessly in the tent, eating into the precious rations as he waited for the weather to change.

The blizzard finally blew itself out on December 9, and later that same evening, Oates shot the last of the horses. They had reached the shadow of the Beardmore Glacier, and Scott ordered the dogs to turn back. Their departure signalled the start of the man-hauling, the remaining 12 men forming three teams for the torturous struggle up the 10,000-foot glacier.

With each sledge weighing over 800 pounds, their progress was excruciatingly laborious. Even the usually indomitable Bowers found it brutal work. "I have never pulled so hard, or so nearly crushed my backbone by the everlasting jerking," he wrote in his diary.

Disappearing into a crevasse was one of the dangers that constantly faced the Antarctic explorers.

On December 13, they covered less than four miles, and Scott was consumed by a deep depression: "A most damnably dismal day...the toil was simply awful."

Another diary had a more upbeat entry for that day: "Our finest day up here...calm most of the day with burning sunshine." The writer was Amundsen, who, at the very moment Scott was dragging his sledge up the Beardmore Glacier, was some 350 miles further south and only a day's march from the South Pole.

Amundsen reaches the Pole

Having set his second departure date for October 19, Amundsen had been frustrated by the weather again, and it wasn't until the following day that he finally managed to strike out from his base. With him were four men he knew would accept his total authority without question: Olav Bjaaland, Helmer Hanssen, Sverre Hassel and Oscar Wisting. They helped him harness 52 dogs to their four 850-pound sledges, said farewell to their colleagues and set off across the Barrier.

The Norwegians made a blistering start, covering 90 miles in only four days. (The British managed 130 miles in the first two weeks.) The men either rode on the sledges or strapped on their skis and let the dogs tow them. They took only six hours to cover their daily mileage, using the rest of their time to sleep, eat and carry out adjustments to clothing and equipment.

On November 1 – the day Scott departed from Cape Evans – Amundsen was 200 miles in front of his rival and going strongly. Shortly after, however, he encountered his first major problem when they strayed into a crevasse field in poor visibility. Hanssen, the expert dog-driver, disappeared into a crevasse and had to be dragged out by his colleagues. "We go with our lives in our

hands each day," wrote Amundsen, "but it's pleasant to hear nobody wants to turn back."

By November 7, they had passed 82°S, where their furthest depot had been placed, and entered unknown territory. Although he betrayed no signs of worry, Amundsen grew increasingly apprehensive as he made his way further south. They had made excellent progress across the Barrier, but before they could look forward to the relative calmness of the polar plateau, they would have to find a way up and through the TransAntarctic Mountains. Amundsen knew that Scott would follow Shackleton's route up the Beardmore Glacier, and he considered it only fair that he should find a different route for himself.

They arrived at the foot of the mountains on November 17 and stared up at the 12,000-foot peaks. It was the critical point in Amundsen's expedition. So far, they had excelled themselves, but all their efforts would be for nothing if they couldn't negotiate a way through the mountains. Adopting the role of the gambler once more, Amundsen led his men up the only route he could find, and for four days they fought their way through "enormous blocks of ice, mighty abysses and wide crevasses" until they reached the plateau. Amundsen had rolled the dice, and they had fallen in his favour.

At this point, the men shot 24 of the remaining 42 dogs, using the flesh to feed themselves and the surviving dogs. It was an unpleasant business, but they knew it was essential if they were to make the final 274 miles to the Pole.

On December 8, they passed Shackleton's record of 1909, the knowledge that they were within 100 miles of their goal injecting fresh life into their weary legs. Five days later, while Scott and his men toiled up the Beardmore Glacier, the Norwegians pitched their tent 15 miles from the Pole. They awoke on the morning of the fourteenth to a fine, clear day. At three o'clock that afternoon, they reached 90°S. Amundsen recorded

Winners: Amundsen (above) photographing sights at the Pole while the dogs have a breather.

Edgar Evans, Oates, Wilson and Scott (above) were later joined by Bowers.

the next few moments in his diary: "I had decided that we would all take part in the historic event... Five roughened, frostbitten fists it was that gripped the post – lifted the fluttering flag on high and planted it together as the very first at the Geographical South Pole." The race had been won.

Runners-up

It took the British polar party 12 days to ascend the Beardmore Glacier, by which time Scott had sent back four more men. Cherry-Garrard, Edward Atkinson, Charles Wright and Patrick Keohane parted company with their remaining eight companions on December 22, 300 miles from the Pole. Cherry-Garrard gave Bowers his handkerchief and handed Wilson his pyjamas before leaving. In return, Wilson entrusted his friend with a letter for his wife. He had finished this by saying, "We are over the worst of it all now and we come home with light loads from depot to depot."

One of the most unpleasant tasks for Scott, as leader, was deciding which men would have to return home as they crept nearer to the Pole: "I dreaded this necessity of choosing – nothing could be more heartrending." Doubtless it also weighed heavily on the minds of the seven men who pulled alongside Scott. For the next two weeks, the two sledge parties hauled their 800-pound loads across the ice, both refusing to give an inch to the other. Scott had said that he would take three men with him to the Pole, and although Oates, Wilson and Petty Officer Evans had been working with him for the past weeks, each of the other four men still harboured a faint hope that he would win a late selection.

Over Christmas and New Year 1912, Scott monitored the performance of all seven of his companions, reaching his decision on the night of January 3. As he entered the other team's tent, Crean was battling with a hacking cough. "You've got a bad cold, Crean," said Scott. The big Irishman knew what was coming: "I understand a half-sung song, sir." Sure enough, Scott had decided to take his sledge party to the Pole. However, there was a surprise in store for Bowers: he would be going as well.

With the Pole only 140 miles away, it was a crushing blow to have to return. "Teddy Evans is terribly disappointed," wrote Scott in his diary, "but he has taken it very well and behaved like a man. Poor old Crean wept and even Lashly was affected."

After the departure of the final support party, a weight appeared to be lifted from Scott's shoulders, and for the next 48 hours his optimism was borne out by some fine weather and good progress. That situation changed on January 6. Temperatures began to drop, and the men

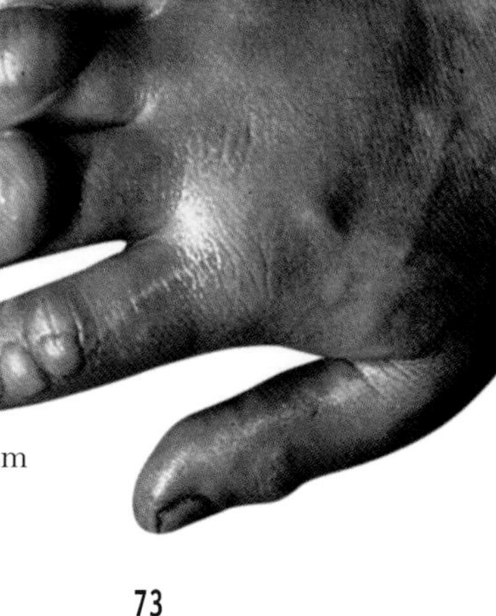

Not a pretty sight: the effects of frostbite on the hand of one of Scott's men.

encountered "bearded" sastrugi and "sandy" patches of snow, caused by persistent showers of ice crystals. Two days later, they were waylaid by a blizzard. When they got going again, on the tenth, Scott noted bitterly, "I have never had such pulling. We have covered six miles [today] but at fearful cost to ourselves."

On the morning of January 16, the five men emerged from a tent pitched only 27 miles north of the Pole. On the previous night, Scott had confided in his diary that they should reach their target the next day, but would they see the appalling sight of the Norwegian flag? By lunchtime, they had covered 7½ miles, and by mid-afternoon another five. Suddenly, Bowers's eyes caught sight of a tiny black speck on the horizon. Scott's diary recorded the next few hours: "We marched on, found that it was a black flag tied to a sledge bearer; near by the remains of a camp; sledge tracks and ski tracks going and coming and the clear trace of dogs' paws – many dogs. This told us the whole story. The Norwegians have forestalled us and are first at the Pole."

"This awful place"

Scott and his men reached the Pole the next day, but they displayed little enthusiasm as they built a small cairn and hoisted the Union Jack. They posed for the obligatory photograph, but the five faces that stared at the camera seemed to bear out Scott's view that the South Pole was an "awful place".

Bowers, however, managed to sound as unremittingly cheerful as ever in a letter to his mother: "Well, here I actually am and very glad to be here too." Wilson simply recorded the events of the day and left little indication of his actual feelings. Oates was the only one of the party who commented on the defeat: "I must say that man [Amundsen] must have had his head screwed on right. The gear they left was in excellent order and

Edgar Evans and Tom Crean (opposite page) two tough men whose strength proved invaluable during the long march towards the Pole.

Amundsen's Tent

Amundsen had left a tent at the South Pole, inside which was a note bearing the names of his four companions and a letter addressed to Scott. It read, "As you are probably the first to reach this area after us, I will ask you kindly to forward this letter to King Haakon VII. If you can use any of the articles left in the tent please do not hesitate to do so. With kind regards I wish you a safe return. Yours Truly, Roald Amundsen." Scott commented in his diary, "I am puzzled at the object." Amundsen's motive for leaving the note has never been revealed: was he taking a precaution in case some tragic accident befell him and his men on their return journey, or was he mocking Scott by underlining who had reached the Pole first?

One of Scott's party inspects Amundsen's tent which contained the enigmatic letter.

The faces of defeat: (left to right) Oates, Scott, Evans, (front row) Bowers and Wilson.

they seem to have had a comfortable trip with their dog teams, very different from our wretched man-hauling."

The five men set out on the 800-mile return journey on January 18. For the first week, Bowers noted that they "sped along merrily" as they recorded a daily average of 20 miles. All of them were suffering, to some extent, from frostbite, but on January 23, Scott noticed that Evans seemed to be unduly troubled by the condition. The normally irrepressible Welshman had withdrawn into his shell, and the stream of good-natured invective that peppered his vocabulary had dried up. "His hands are really bad," noted Scott, "and to my surprise he shows sign of losing heart over it."

Of all the British explorers, he had been most devastated by the sight of the Norwegian flag. As the only working-class member of the polar party, he had hoped that the cachet of being one of the first men to the South Pole would have provided financial security for himself and his family for the rest of their lives. He found the bitter pill of defeat difficult to swallow.

Scott (right) could do nothing as first Evans and then Oates succumbed to their injuries.

Evans's plight steadily worsened, and the discovery on February 7 that a day's biscuit ration was missing caused his morale to drop further. At least, by then, they were off the polar plateau and beginning to descend the Beardmore Glacier, which they hoped would mean an increase in temperature and a better sledging surface when they reached the Barrier at the bottom.

There was no relief for Evans, however; yet he refused to become a passenger on the sledge. On February 15, they managed 15 miles, although the cost to Evans became apparent on the following day, when he collapsed in the late afternoon. The next morning he insisted on pulling his share of the load but soon after starting out, he began to have trouble with his ski shoes and he repeatedly asked for a halt so he could adjust them. A short while later, Evans collapsed again, but this time never regained consciousness.

The loss of Evans was a sad blow for his four companions, but the most distressing aspect of his death had been his mental decline. "It's an extraordinary thing about Evans," Oates wrote in his diary. "He's lost his guts and behaves like an old woman." Oates and Evans had never been particularly close, but that wasn't the reason for this outburst. The former was aware that his own physical condition was deteriorating fast, and it was unlikely that he would survive much longer. Evans's breakdown frightened him, not because he feared death, but because he knew it was his turn next and he wanted to die with dignity, like an officer and a gentleman.

The death of Oates

Oates had suffered from bad feet for weeks before he reached the Pole. Shortly before Christmas, he had written in his diary, "My feet are giving me a lot of trouble. They have been continually wet since leaving Hut Point and now walking along this hard ice in frozen crampons has rather made hay of them."

Another problem was also affecting Oates: his old war wound. He had been recommended for a Victoria Cross during the Boer War, after refusing to surrender his position despite being severely wounded in the left thigh. The endless miles of marching through thick snow and across hard ice had caused the wound to flare up once more.

His closest friend on the expedition was Edward Atkinson, who sensed that Oates had had enough by the time they reached the top of the Beardmore Glacier. He had done all that had been required of him with regard to the ponies - the reason he had been brought south in the first place - and he had little personal ambition to reach the Pole. The only thought that prevented Oates from disclosing his reluctance to continue was that his regiment and "perhaps the whole army" would be pleased if he reached the Pole.

Scott's attitude to Oates compounded the situation. Of all the men who ever came under Scott's command, the upper-class cavalry officer was the only one who could flagrantly question his orders and not incur his wrath. Scott liked and respected Oates – although at times these feelings weren't reciprocated – and in particular derived strength from the fact that he never became

And we did not leave him
till 2 hours after his
death – We knew that
poor Oates was walking to
his death but though we
tried to dissuade him we
knew it was the act of
a brave man and an
English gentleman.
We all hope to meet the
end with a similar spirit
and assuredly the end is
not far.
I can only write at lunch
& then only occasionally. The
cold is intense -40 at
midday – My companions
are unendingly cheerful
but we are all on the
verge of serious frostbites –
and though we constantly
talk of fetching through

perturbed. Oates's self-confidence and steadfastness were reassuring, and it probably never entered Scott's mind that he was unfit to continue.

By the end of January, however, Oates's big toe had turned blue-black and his nose and cheeks had been coloured yellow by frostbite. For the next month, he soldiered on, his companions being unaware that his feet were nearly dead from gangrene. On March 2, the pain became too much and he asked Wilson to dress his feet. Scott was horrified by their "wretched condition".

On March 6, Scott marvelled at Oates's pluck and noted that he never once complained as he dragged each foot forward. The next day, however, Scott wrote in his diary that Oates's crisis was near. Oates knew it, too, and he must also have known that he was being backed into a corner from which there was no escape. Before he had embarked on the trek to the Pole, he and some of his fellow explorers had discussed the appropriate course of action should a member of the polar party imperil the lives of his comrades. Oates had been adamant about what should be done. He thought a pistol should be taken on the sledge and "if anyone breaks down he should have the privilege of using it".

Unfortunately, Oates had no pistol. The only other easy method was opium tablets, but that wasn't the correct way for a cavalry officer to die. On March 10, Oates asked Wilson about his chances and received a fudged answer. "He practically asked for advice," Scott recorded on the following day.

Five days later, the temperature was -43°F and Oates could take no more. He asked to be left in his sleeping bag, but his companions refused, even though they knew he was hindering their own progress. He went to sleep on the night of March 16, hoping not to wake the next morning – his thirty-second birthday – but he did.

Struggling to his feet, Oates opened the flap of the tent and turned to his colleagues: "I am just going outside and may be some time."

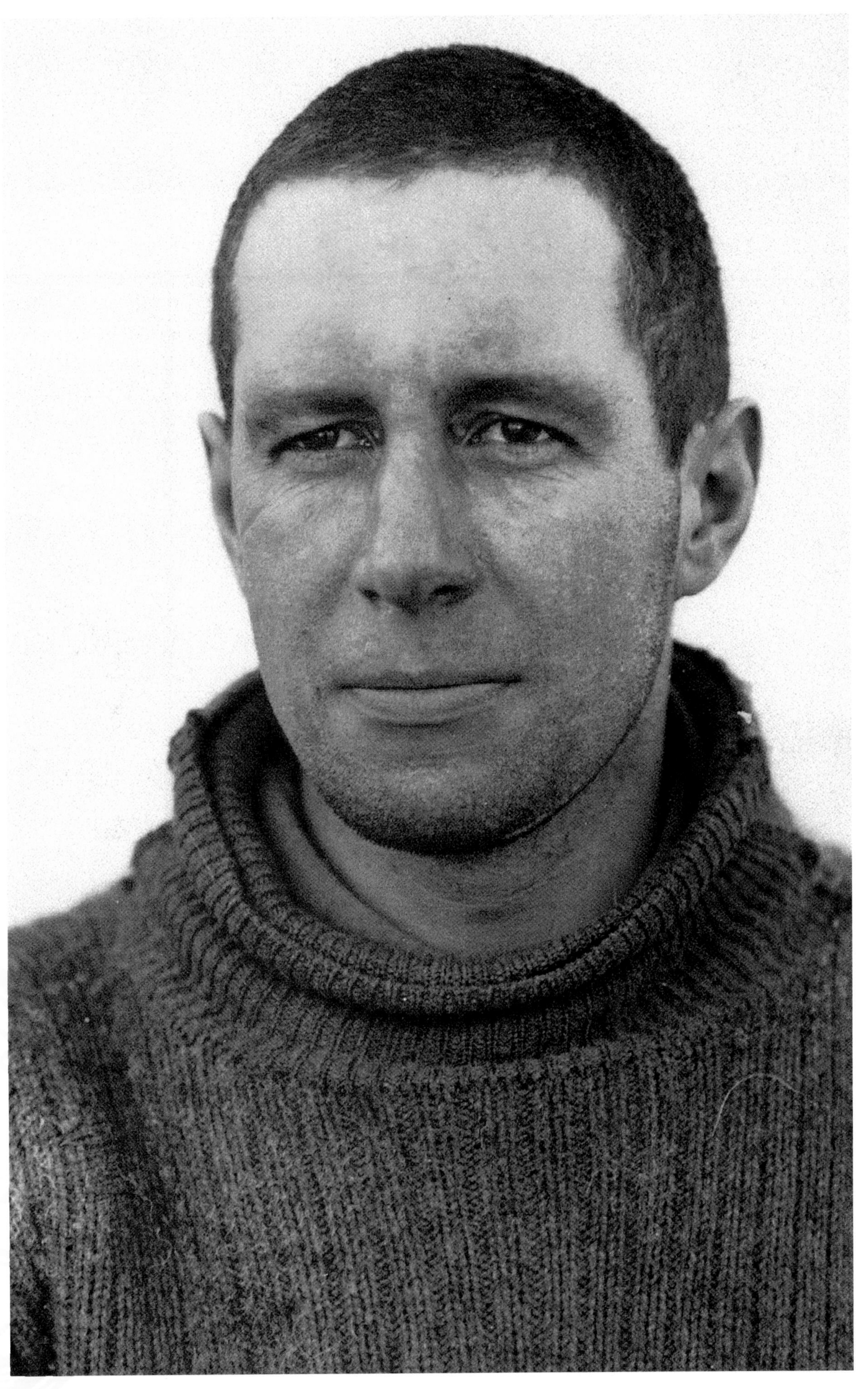

Captain Oates's last words – "I am just going outside and may be some time" – were later learned by generations of British schoolchildren.

The entry in Scott's diary recording the death of Captain Oates.

The end of the road

"We knew that poor Oates was walking to his death," Scott wrote, hours after the man had left the tent, "but though we tried to dissuade him, we knew it was the act of a brave man and an English gentleman."

Scott and his two remaining companions also knew that Oates's self-sacrifice had considerably improved their own chances of reaching One Ton Depot, a little under 50 miles to the north, where food and fuel awaited them. By now, Scott's feet were so badly frostbitten that his right foot would require amputation if they made it back to Hut Point. But could they make it? Scott wrote that Bowers was "unendingly cheerful...still confident of getting through."

On March 18, the three were only 21 miles from the depot, and salvation seemed to be within their grasp. Three days later, the Antarctic weather ripped it from their hands. A seething blizzard descended, and they were held captive in their tent as the wind roared around them. Scott knew that the game was up on March 23, when he wrote, "Have decided it shall be natural – we shall march for the depot with or without our effects and die in our tracks."

However, the storm outside refused even to allow them the honour of dying on the march, and for the next week all they could do was lie in their tent and wait for death to call. The final entry in Scott's journal was made on March 29. He had written 12 letters as he waited to die, including one addressed to the public. He finished this by saying, "Had we lived, I should have had a tale to tell of the hardihood, endurance and courage of my companions which would have stirred the heart of every Englishman. These rough notes and our dead bodies must tell the tale."

Norwegian Success

On March 21 – the day Scott, Wilson and Bowers were pitching their tent for the last time – Roald Amundsen was leaving Tasmania for the Australian mainland and the start of his grand Antarctic lecture tour.

Amundsen and his four companions had reached the safety of their base on January 26, 1912, without having experienced any hitches on their return from the Pole. They had covered the 1,400 miles in only 99 days; frostbite, hunger and exhaustion had never entered their tent.

When Amundsen's diary for his return journey was compared with that of his dead British rival, it highlighted dramatically the contrasting fortunes of the two parties. On December 21, the Norwegians increased their daily ration from 350 grams per man to 400 grams. The remaining 13 dogs sprinted across the polar plateau with reckless abandon, and the men welcomed the New Year with another 50-gram increase in their daily food allowance.

The five crept up to their base in the early hours of January 26, surprising their sleeping colleagues with the speed of their return. As they gathered around a table to enjoy some coffee, Amundsen informed the men who had stayed behind that the explorers hadn't "much to tell in the way of privation or great struggle. The whole thing went like a dream."

Amundsen's expedition was a masterpiece of precise planning. Certainly, he enjoyed some good luck along the way, but his whole strategy had been brilliantly executed: his accurate assessment of the Bay of Whales as a suitable base; the use of dogs; men who were experts on skis; the calculated approach to ration allowance; and the series of well-stocked depots at every degree of latitude. On January 30, Amundsen left Antarctica to tell the world about his success.

The search party

The first intimation that tragedy could be close at hand came on February 19, when Crean staggered into Hut Point with the news that Lieutenant Evans was dying of scurvy 30 miles to the south. Evans was rescued and made a full recovery, but his rapid deterioration was an ominous sign. Lashly had detected signs of scurvy only three weeks after they had waved Scott goodbye, and it was only his diligent nursing and Crean's courage in making the final march for help that saved Evans's life.

The master planner: Amundsen's conquest of the South Pole went, in his own words, 'like a dream'.

The memorial to Captain Scott and his men erected in Antarctica by the survivors of the Terra Nova *expedition.*

With this in mind, Cherry-Garrard took a team of dogs as far as One Ton Depot on February 26. Atkinson, who had assumed command following Evans's illness, told Cherry-Garrard to "judge what to do" if he arrived at the depot and found no trace of the polar party. However, Cherry-Garrard was also reminded that Scott had left clear instructions that the dogs were not to be risked, for they were needed for work the following summer.

Cherry-Garrard reached the depot on March 3 to find it deserted. This left him with an unenviable choice: head south in search of the party or sit and wait. With no dog food at the depot, the only way that the animals could continue south was by feeding on one another. Mindful of Scott's assertion that the dogs were needed for the following season, and also concerned that the appalling weather on the Barrier could lead to the two parties missing each other, he pitched his tent and waited. On March 10, with supplies running short, he headed back to Cape Evans.

Later, after Cherry-Garrard discovered that as he turned north, only 60 miles to the south, Oates was approaching death, he became immersed in guilt that remained with him for the rest of his life. Twenty years later, he still suffered a recurring nightmare: "I am asleep in my bunk; the door opens, letting in its mist of cold air, and the polar party walks in, shaking the snow from their clothes and the ice from their faces. The disappointment of finding that it is only a dream will last for days."

By mid-April, the 13 men at Cape Evans had accepted that the polar party had perished on the ice. Winter prevented any immediate search attempts, so it wasn't until the end of October that an 11-man search party set out to try to find the bodies of their five companions.

On November 12, shortly before midday, one of the men spotted what he took to be a cairn. On closer inspection, it turned out to be Scott's tent. Atkinson and Lashly beat the snow from the canvas and crawled inside. Scott was between his two faithful friends. On his left was Wilson, while Bowers lay on his right. Both looked as though they had slipped away peacefully. Scott, on the other hand, appeared to have fought death to the very last. Cherry-Garrard described how Scott had "thrown back the flaps of his bag at the end. His left hand was stretched over Wilson."

Atkinson read Scott's diary and assembled the men to tell them what had happened. Then they collapsed the tent and built a cairn in remembrance of the three explorers. The next day, they went in search of Oates's body, but found only his socks and finnesko. Near the spot where he had made his final gesture, a cross was erected and a note attached commemorating "a very gallant gentleman".

What went wrong?

When news of the tragedy reached the outside world, in early 1913, the British newspapers proclaimed the men's deaths as a glorious example of English heroism. There wasn't a dissenting voice. No one asked if Scott's death, and that of his companions, could have been avoided. No one questioned why the British expedition went so wrong, when the Norwegians enjoyed a cake-walk.

"We took risks," Scott confessed in his Message to the Public, "we knew we took them: things have come out against us, and therefore we have no cause for complaint." He didn't shy away, however, from listing his excuses: Evans's "astonishing failure", the weather, the ponies and the "sickening" of Oates. Scott's message set out the reasons for their deaths and how little could have been done to prevent the tragedy, but it evaded the matter of his mistakes.

The 1913 London memorial service to the five men who died on their return from the South Pole.

Relics of Scott's expedition on display at Earls Court, London, in June 1913.

Provision
BAG

It was true that they had been unlucky with the weather, experiencing unseasonally cold temperatures on the Barrier and encountering two blizzards that confined them to their tents, the first for four days and the second much longer. Yet on February 8, as they descended the Beardmore Glacier, Scott took advantage of some fine weather to collect rock samples for scientific research. The five of them spent an afternoon gathering 35 pounds of rocks, when they could have edged a vital few miles further north towards safety.

One of the consequences of that first blizzard at the foot of the Beardmore Glacier was that the men began eating into the rations that had been meant for the ascent. This was the first step on the road to growing hunger and diminished strength for the five who made the final dash to the Pole. The second step was when Scott decided, at the last minute, to increase the Polar party from four men to five. Bowers's presence threw into disarray all the plans and calculations that had been made on the assumption that four men would constitute the final team.

That's not to say that Bowers shouldn't have been in the Polar party. He was the fittest man on Scott's expedition, and it was a correct decision to include him. But why didn't Scott send Oates or Evans back? Oates had been limping since the Beardmore Glacier, and Wilson had told Scott long before he announced the final party that Lashly was in better shape than Evans. Scott wouldn't listen. Oates and Evans were a source of strength to him, and he believed them both to be nigh on indestructible.

However, Scott might have saved himself and the others if he had taken Oates's advice during the laying of One Ton Depot. Oates had implored his leader to push south for another 30 miles before shooting the horses and depoting their meat for the return of the polar party in the following year. Scott had refused, saying that it was too cruel. Oates told him he would regret this decision. Scott and his two companions died 11 miles short of One Ton Depot. If he had listened to Oates, he would have reached the depot three days before the fatal blizzard struck.

Scott made many mistakes during the expedition, but with hindsight it is easy to criticize. Given that he was suffering from the debilitating effects of exhaustion, hunger and

frostbite, one can hardly lay the blame for the tragedy solely at his feet. Scott had his flaws – and he was aware of them – but he was also a man of integrity, loyalty and courage. There is no question that if he had deserted Evans and Oates when they became a hindrance, he would have survived. But a man who will not tolerate cruelty to horses is not one who will leave a companion to die. Would Amundsen, the ruthlessly efficient professional explorer, have jeopardized his life for the sake of a dying comrade?

Children play at the base of Scott's statue in Christchuch, New Zealand.

CHAPTER FIVE

Endurance

With the race to the South Pole having been won, Shackleton expanded his horizons and announced an expedition to cross the Antarctic continent on foot. Unfazed by those who said that his plan was mad, in August 1914 he sailed from England in the Endurance *to embark upon what would become one of the greatest stories of survival against overwhelming odds.*

Winston Churchill in 1915 and (opposite) the Endurance *at night.*

"The first crossing of the Antarctic continent, from sea to sea via the Pole, apart from its historic value, will be a journey of great scientific importance."

With these words, Sir Ernest Shackleton unveiled his latest venture. The Imperial Transantarctic Expedition was his boldest bid yet for glory. He planned to begin the 1,800-mile trek on the coastline of the Weddell Sea, from where he and five men would cross a great swathe of unmapped Antarctica on their way to the Pole. Once there, they would follow the route he had pioneered during the *Nimrod* expedition.

Shackleton announced the expedition on December 29, 1913, and immediately it was greeted with scepticism and even scorn. "The Pole has already been discovered," roared a young Admiralty Lord called Winston Churchill, "what is the point of another expedition?"

Churchill had made a valid point. What was the use of Shackleton's expedition now that

the Pole had been discovered and five British explorers had lost their lives in the pursuit of that goal? Shackleton had anticipated this question and was ready with an answer. "Every step will be an advance in geographical science," he said. "It will be learned whether the great Victorian chain of mountains, which has been traced from the Ross Sea to the Pole, extends across the continent and thus links up with the Andes of South America."

However, no matter how much he tried to convince people that he was going south for science, Shackleton's real motive was plain for the world to see: adventure. After his return from the *Nimrod* expedition, he had wallowed in the fame that followed. An audience with King Edward VII, invitations to speak at the Albert Hall, the darling of the newspapers – Shackleton loved the celebrity lifestyle, and he blazed his way through European and American lecture tours.

Then the journalists stopped taking an interest in him, and Shackleton's star began to wane. It was back to the monotony of everyday life and the role of husband and father. What made the transition even more difficult was the news of Scott's race to the Pole with Amundsen. Shackleton's role was off-stage, restricted to providing commentary and observations for the press.

Shackleton returned to the world of business, but he enjoyed no more success than in his earlier years. His plans to become a gold prospector in Hungary came to nothing, and a scheme of his brother's that he hoped would make him rich ended in a similarly depressing fashion. It was time to launch another expedition.

The catalyst for the Transantarctic Expedition was the German explorer Wilhelm Filchner. At the beginning of 1913, he had returned to Europe after an unsuccessful attempt to cross the Antarctic continent. The expedition wasn't a total failure, however, for Filchner had discovered a huge ice shelf in the Weddell Sea. Although he hadn't managed to establish a base of the shelf [now called the Filchner Ice Shelf], he told Shackleton that he believed it was a suitable point for launching a transantarctic expedition.

This was music to Shackleton's ears. With the prospect of another trip south, he became his old self again, buoyed with enthusiasm and determination. The trusty Frank Wild was appointed second-in-command, and an exuberant New Zealander called Frank Worsley was offered the command of the expedition's ship. Shackleton had been adamant that he wouldn't settle for a vessel as decrepit as *Nimrod* and, eventually, bought a good-looking 300-ton ship called *Polaris* from a Norwegian yard. He renamed her *Endurance*.

Eager recruits queue in London for a war they thought would be over by Christmas.

War or ice?

Shackleton and his ship were due at the Cowes yachting regatta in the first week of August, where a visit from King George V had been promised. Unfortunately, the inspection never materialized; the King had more pressing matters to deal with. For some years, Europe had been quietly smouldering with political differences and historical grievances. The assassination of Archduke Franz Ferdinand, in June 1914, ignited the continent, and soon most of the world would be engulfed by war.

On the morning of August 4, *Endurance* was moored at Southend when Shackleton heard the announcement he had feared: Britain had declared war on Germany. He mustered his men on deck and broke the news. Then he said that he hoped there would be no objection if he offered the ship and the services of all 28 men to the Royal Navy.

There was not a murmur of complaint from the crew, and a telegram was duly dispatched to the Admiralty with a codicil attached. "We only asked," wrote Shackleton later, "that the expedition

might be considered as a single unit...there were enough trained and experienced men amongst us to man a destroyer." Shackleton received a one-word reply an hour later: "Proceed." The Antarctic beckoned.

In the introduction to *South*, his book describing the expedition, Shackleton repeatedly referred the reader to his offer of the ship and men to the Admiralty when war was declared. This stemmed from a certain amount of criticism directed at the crew when they eventually returned to Britain, at the end of 1916. By then, hundreds of thousands of British servicemen had been slaughtered in the war, and there was a feeling in some quarters that Shackleton and his men had shirked their duty by going south. This was unfair.

Some of the crew of Endurance *in good spirits shortly before sailing south.*

When war broke out in the summer of 1914, the whole country expected the fighting to be over by Christmas. As Shackleton said, "Few thought the war would last through five years and involve the whole world."

On Saturday August 8, *Endurance* left the war behind and, after a brief stop in Buenos Aires, arrived at South Georgia in November, 1914. The island was uninhabited save for a Norwegian whaling community, the members of which were happy to provide Shackleton with their knowledge of the surrounding waters. The news wasn't good. The ice was not only exceptionally severe for the time of year, but it had also crept much further north than usual. These were ominous signs in a sea that Shackleton described as "notoriously inhospitable".

The wake of Endurance *as she sails south through the ice.*

On December 5 *Endurance* sailed from South Georgia and headed in a south-easterly direction toward the South Sandwich Islands. Two days later, on December 7, they spotted icebergs, and that evening ice was gripping the hull of *Endurance*. The situation didn't improve, and a week before Christmas, Shackleton noted that they were encountering pack ice of a "very obstinate character".

A month later, *Endurance* became trapped in the ice. Over the next few weeks, repeated attempts were made to free the ship, but with winter approaching, and the resultant drop in temperature, Shackleton realized that there would be no immediate escape from the snare. *Endurance* and its crew were at the mercy of the drifting pack ice. "Where will the vagrant winds and currents carry the ship during the long winter months that are ahead of us? We will go west, no doubt, but how far?"

Trapped

"The idea of spending winter in an ice-bound ship is extremely unpleasant," wrote Frank Hurley, the photographer on the *Endurance*, when their predicament became apparent. It was a view shared by all the men, and Shackleton knew that he had to act swiftly and decisively lest morale was destroyed.

By the end of February, the ship had been turned into a winter station, the men having divided the living quarters into cubicles. "The Billabong", "The Nuts" and "The Anchorage" were among the names given to their new homes.

New accommodation was also provided for the dogs, which were disembarked and housed in their kennels on the ice. Six dog teams were formed, and regular competitions between them helped exercise both man and beast. On June 15, the first Antarctic Dog Derby was run, there being a flurry of pre-race gambling with chocolate and cigarettes as the stakes.

Hussey and Hurley, on nightwatch aboard the trapped Endurance, *pass the time with a game of chess.*

The entrapment of *Endurance* was the sort of crisis that Shackleton thrived on, and his leadership was crucial to maintaining the men's morale. "We seem to be a wonderfully happy family," wrote Thomas Orde-Lees. "But I think Sir Ernest is the real secret behind our unanimity."

Football matches were a common sight on the ice when light permitted. "The rules were not always observed," said Frank Worsley. "Once I saw three men sitting on the referee, rubbing his nose into the snow. What would the Football Association say?" Shackleton also encouraged the men to practise using their skis, and he welcomed trips across the ice to investigate icebergs and other features that caught their attention.

Shackleton's greatest test was the onset of the winter months. On May 8, the sun disappeared and would not reappear until late July. He remembered the breakdown of discipline during the *Belgica* expedition in 1898, when the ship became trapped by ice in the Bellingshausen Sea and several men lost their sanity in the months of darkness. Therefore he insisted on rigid discipline. No crew member was allowed to let his hair grow below his

Football crazy: one of the most popular ways of passing the time of day.

collar, and punctuality was expected at meal times. "Breakfast was at 9am sharp," recalled Hurley, "else woe betide."

The sun returned on July 26, 79 days after slipping out of view, and for a short while the men's morale lifted along with the darkness. By the beginning of August, however, the ice began to tighten the noose around the *Endurance*. "The effects of the pressure around us were awe-inspiring," wrote Shackleton. "Mighty blocks of ice, gripped between melting floes, rose slowly till they jumped like cherry stones squeezed between thumb and finger."

The ship's routine was continued throughout August, but as September arrived, the roar of the ice seemed to intensify. Shackleton realized that the ship was doomed, and it was a question of when, rather than if, the *Endurance* would sink. Worsley shared his commander's view, but he was amazed that the vessel had lasted as long as she had. "She has been strained, her beams arched upwards by the fearful pressure, her very sides opened and closed again as she was actually bent and curved along her length; groaning like a living thing."

By October 18, *Endurance* had keeled over and

was listing 30 degrees to port. Six days later, she sprang a leak, and Shackleton ordered their supplies to be moved on to the ice. The next day, having been locked in the ice for 281 days and drifted 573 miles to the north-west, he finally gave the order to abandon ship. "The task is to reach land with all the members of the expedition," wrote Shackleton. The nearest land with food and shelter, however, was 374 miles away.

Adrift on the ice

Shackleton passed the first night adrift on the ice, pacing up and down in the shadow of *Endurance* and ruminating on their dilemma. At first light, together with Wild and Hurley, he boiled some hot milk and went from tent to tent, dishing it out to the men. They received little in the way of gratitude. "If any of you gentlemen would like your boots cleaned," said a disgruntled Wild to the occupants of one tent, "just put them outside!"

Later that morning, Shackleton assembled the men and explained his plan. They would march over 300 miles north-west towards Snow Hill, where they would find food and shelter. It was a bold scheme, but one that hadn't been born out of necessity. After all, they had salvaged 56 days' worth of full rations, and there was no shortage of seals and penguins to slaughter. They could have sat and waited for the drift of the pack ice to lead them to open water. However, Shackleton had another reason for keeping on the move: "It will be much better for the men in general to feel that, even though progress is slow, they are on their way to land than it will be simply to sit down and wait for the tardy north-westerly drift to take us out of this cruel waste of ice."

They stripped the *Endurance* of all essential items – Shackleton limited each man to no more than two pounds of personal effects – and began hauling the lifeboats across the ice. Surmounting the myriad pressure ridges was back-breaking work, and three days later Shackleton called a halt. They rested on a floe of ice measuring one mile square – which they christened Ocean Camp – and there they remained for the next two months.

December brought the summer and an increase in temperature. A surface thaw threatened to break up their floe and send parts of Ocean Camp floating off in different directions. Thus, on December 23, they broke camp and began hauling the boats across the ice once more. However, the going was even worse than before, and for

Some of the expedition's dogs bear witness to the death throes of Endurance.

Killer whales

Throughout the period Shackleton and his men were adrift on the floe, they were surrounded by killer whales. These fearsome beasts grow to 30 feet in length and have a mouth with a four-foot stretch. Killer whales hunt in packs and, although not man-eaters by nature, they may fail to distinguish between humans and seals. Their method of hunting involves a mixture of stealth and brute force. Worsley described how a killer whale would select its victim: "A lizard-like head would show while the killer gazed along the floe with wicked eyes." Then it would submerge, locate the spot to attack and use its powerful back to break through the ice and grab its quarry. Shackleton recalled seeing a killer whale leave a twelve- by eight-foot hole after smashing through ice a foot thick.

McNeish, the carpenter, the effort outweighed the reward. It had taken them four days to cover six miles. He refused to continue. Shackleton was faced with mutiny. He defused the situation with a mixture of diplomacy and optimism, convincing the men that he knew what he was doing. Then he took McNeish aside and told him to behave himself. The word "pistol" was mentioned; McNeish got the message.

McNeish's rebellion had disturbed Shackleton, not only because of the challenge to his authority, but also because the Scot was right. Shackleton was pushing them to do the impossible. At the end of December, they established a new base on the ice – Patience Camp – and there they stayed as January passed into February and they continued their average drift of a mile a day. "We have an increasing desire to get firm ground under our feet," wrote Shackleton, as April arrived. "The floe has been a good friend to us, but it is liable any time now to break up and fling us into the unplumbed sea."

On April 7, they sighted a "beacon of safety" – the peaks of Clarence Island and Elephant Island, 60 miles to the north-west. Two days later, the

men said goodbye to the ice that had been their home for the previous six months and launched the three boats.

"Bale! Bale like hell!"

"It is to be hoped the south-east breeze will hold and so save us from drifting east of Clarence Island," Frank Worsley wrote in his log on Sunday, April 9, 1915. This understated entry belied the daunting prospect facing the 28 men as they clambered into the boats.

Worsley held the lives of all the men in his hands. They were pinning their hopes on his ability to navigate the 60 miles to Elephant Island, through rough seas and strong winds. Although Worsley had a sextant with him, he didn't enjoy the benefit of the sun and had to rely on dead reckoning to determine their course. "I can never forget my acute anxiety," he wrote later. "If there was a mistake in my sights, 28 men would have sailed out to death."

His apprehension was understandable. Elephant Island was an uninhabited and desolate pinprick of land, measuring 25 by 15 miles, in a huge ocean.

Adrift on a floe (inset) while (above) Shackleton, with hat, directs the pulling of one of the sledges.

(Overleaf) Shackleton and Wild (foreground) and the other members of Endurance *at Ocean camp.*

Frank Worsley: the boisterous Kiwi was to prove himself a brilliant navigator.

Clarence Island, its neighbour, was just as bleak. If Worsley blundered in his navigation and they drifted east of the two islands, they would be pushed out into the open sea and would die from starvation, cold or drowning.

After three days at sea, Worsley caught a brief glimpse of the sun and snapped their position to discover how far they had sailed. They had been pushed back 30 miles to the east. It was a devastating blow, but Shackleton hid it from the men. "We haven't done as well as we expected," was all he would say.

The next 48 hours punished the men. Morale plummeted along with the temperature as they struggled to make headway against strong currents. The cold penetrated their very souls and, when they weren't rowing, groups would huddle together for warmth in the bottoms of the boats, oblivious to the snow showers that covered their bodies with a white sheen. At least rowing gave the men a chance to warm up, and long after the experience, Shackleton remembered how the "Burberry suits of the rowers crackled as the men bent to the oars; little fragments of ice frost falling from arms and bodies".

On April 14, they had been at sea for six days. Elephant Island was less than 20 miles away, and an end to their suffering seemed to be in sight. The weather had other ideas. That night, a gale blew up, and Worsley and his crew in the *Dudley Docker* found themselves fighting for their lives. "Bale! Bale like hell!" screamed Worsley, as waves swamped their little boat. Orde-Lees, who had lain seasick at the bottom of the boat for the past week, suddenly sprang into action and spent hour after hour baling water while vomiting repeatedly.

At dawn on the morning of April 15, the gale departed as quickly as it had arrived, and the three boats nipped through a reef to reach the sanctuary of Elephant Island. Most of the men hadn't slept for a week, and few had eaten more than a few pieces of raw seal meat during that time. As they stumbled up the beach – the first time they had stood on land since December 5, 1914 – Shackleton surveyed the sheer cliffs that seemed to glare angrily down at them. He knew their ordeal was far from over. "I decided not to share with the men the knowledge of the uncertainties of our situation until they had enjoyed the full sweetness of rest untroubled by the thought that at any minute they might be called to face peril again."

The landing on Elephant Island was the first time the men had set foot on land for 18 months.

Time for a brew for some of Endurance*'s crew after their safe arrival on Elephant Island.*

The *James Caird*

"Why would anyone look for us here?" That was the first question Shackleton asked himself when he jumped off the *James Caird* and on to Elephant Island. Any search party would concentrate their efforts on the southern reaches of the Weddell Sea and never think of looking so far north.

Shackleton was also becoming increasingly concerned about some of the men's sanity. "Privation and exposure had left their mark on the party, and the health and mental condition of several men were causing me serious anxiety."

After consulting Wild and Worsley, Shackleton announced a plan. He and five men would sail the 22-foot *James Caird* 800 miles to South Georgia and fetch a ship to rescue those who remained on Elephant Island. Shackleton outlined this intention as though he was talking about an afternoon cruise on the Thames. But despite his calm demeanour, he knew what awaited him. "The ocean south of Cape

Horn," he wrote, "is known to be the most tempestuous storm-swept area of water in the world."

Shackleton and the five men he selected – Crean, Worsley, John Vincent, Harry McNeish and Tim McCarthy – set sail on April 24 with two masts and four oars to help them cross the 800 miles of ocean. At first, the sea was unusually calm, as if it was toying with the *James Caird* and waiting for the moment to strike. Sure enough, on the following day, the waves rose, and for two weeks the six men were subjected to a chilling catalogue of hardship and deprivation.

The men's skin was rubbed red raw by the waves that continually crashed over the boat. Salt water invaded their sores, causing them to fester and weep. There was no escape when they went below, for the icy water had infiltrated the boat's tiny cabin. Worsley described the ordeal of entering their sleeping bags: "It felt like getting between frozen rawhide. You kicked your feet violently together to warm them and the bag, then slid in to the waist. At first, while you knocked your feet together, it felt like an icehouse, and then it began to thaw out and you wished it hadn't."

By the end of the first week, the *James Caird* was covered in 15 inches of ice, and the boat began to lose its resilience. "She had become more like a log than a boat," wrote Shackleton. Each day, the men would take it in turns to crawl along the deck and hack the ice off with an axe. It was terrifying work, for the waves did their utmost to dislodge them.

The nadir came just after midnight on May 6, when Shackleton was alone up top, steering the boat through some rough weather. Peering through the darkness, he thought he saw a line of clear sky to the south-west. "I called to the men that the sky was clearing, and then a moment later realized that what I had seen was not a rift in the clouds but the white crest of an enormous wave." It was the biggest wave Shackleton had encountered in his 26 years at sea. He had just enough time to yell a warning, "For God's sake, hold on! It's got us," before the *James Caird* was swallowed up by thousands of tons of churning water.

The boat lurched and sagged under the weight of the wave but miraculously she remained upright. For the next ten minutes, Shackleton and his companions baled for their lives until the *James Caird* slowly rose back to life. For the time being, they were safe, but it had been a moment of sheer terror for the six men. Vincent had suffered a breakdown and was no longer of practical use. The remainder would go the same way unless they could reach South Georgia.

(Overleaf) The crew of the James Caird *embark on their 800 mile journey, across the world's most dangerous sea, to South Georgia.*

The men left behind on Elephant Island wave goodbye as the James Caird disappears into the distance.

Hurricane

On May 7, Worsley estimated that they were 80 miles from South Georgia. It had been a remarkable feat of navigation. Throughout the voyage, the sun had peeped out from behind the clouds for a few seconds two or three times a week. When it showed itself, Worsley had to be waiting with his sextant: "If ready for it, and smart, I caught it. The procedure was: I peered out from under our burrow – precious sextant cuddled under my chest to prevent seas falling on it. Sir Ernest stood by under the canvas with chronometer, pencil and book. I shouted, 'Stand by,' and knelt on the thwart – two men holding me up on either side. I brought the sun down to where the horizon ought to be and as the boat leaped frantically upward on the crest of a wave, snapped a good guess at the altitude and yelled, 'Stop.'"

In this haphazard fashion, Worsley had guided them over 700 miles and almost to within sight of their goal. Now they had to make a choice. Should they head for the whaling station on the north-east coast of South Georgia, where food and warm beds awaited them, or should they seek a landing on the uninhabited south-west side of the island? Thirst and exhaustion cried out for the whaling station, but Shackleton knew that poor visibility and prevailing westerlies could combine to push them

east of the northern coast, out into the open sea and oblivion. He decided to play safe and changed course for the barren southern side of the island.

At noon on May 8, the snow-capped crags of South Georgia were spotted. Shackleton considered it too dangerous to attempt a landing in the gathering gloom and gave the order to stand off until morning. It was frustrating for the men, but at least as they hove-to 18 miles from shore, they knew they were safe. They had taken on the might of the world's deadliest ocean and won. But the sea had one final card to play.

The groaning of the wind increased steadily during the night, and by the next morning it was shrieking with all its might. By noon, they were in the teeth of a hurricane and the *James Caird* was taking on water quicker than the men could bale it. She was also being driven progressively closer to the rocks of South Georgia. "It looked as though we were doomed," recalled Worsley, "past the skill of man to save." With every gigantic wave, the boat was swept upwards, then seemed to totter on top of a mass of seething water, at the mercy of the hysterical wind, before crashing into the hollow below where, for a brief eerie moment, she seemed almost becalmed.

In the midst of the mayhem, Worsley contemplated death and was struck by a pang of

The imposing peaks of South Georgia were welcomed by the crew of James Caird.

regret "for having brought my diary and annoyance that no one would ever know we had got so far". It seemed unbearably cruel that their loved ones would never know how hard they had battled for their lives since leaving England nearly two years before.

Suddenly, the wind shifted direction, as if it had tired of playing the deadly game. The *James Caird* had been only feet from the rocks, but now it was possible for Worsley to change sails and steer them clear of danger. "I have marvelled often," Shackleton wrote later of this moment, "at the thin line that divides success from failure and the sudden turn that leads from apparently certain disaster to comparative safety."

Across South Georgia

The six men sailed into King Haakon Bay and discovered a little cove. They spilled out of the *James Caird* as if they were reeling drunk. Their feet had become numb with the constant cold, and it took them several minutes to find their land legs. Vincent and McNeish were in an appalling condition and would have been lucky to survive another 24 hours at sea.

They spent the next ten days recuperating from their ordeal. Crean used some baby albatrosses to cook an endless supply of delicious hoosh, and slowly life and vigour returned to their bodies. Leaving McNeish, Vincent and McCarthy with the boat, Shackleton, Worsley and Crean set off for the whaling station at Stromness.

With his unique blend of unflagging optimism and self-belief, Shackleton led his two companions up into the mountains early on the morning of May 19, as if he didn't have a care in the world. Although they were only 20 miles from Stromness, they were absurdly ill-equipped for a hike through uncharted mountains. Shackleton had their only ice axe, while their rotting shoes and tattered Burberry clothes would be of little use in the terrain they would be traversing.

Once again, the task of navigation fell to Worsley, but with no accurate map to help him, he had to rely on guesswork. A few hours after setting out, they found their way blocked by a mountain

range of five forbidding ridges. Three times Shackleton led them wearily to the tops of 4,000-foot ridges, only to discover that the other side was pitted with treacherous crevasses and precipices. Morale dropped lower every time they were forced to retrace their steps and try another route.

Eventually, they reached the fourth ridge as dusk descended and, again, found that there was no obvious way forward. As they discussed their next move, a blanket of freezing fog rolled in and began to obscure their view. Shackleton knew that he had to act quickly. After all they had been through in

Frank Worsley's handwritten map detailing the route across South Georgia.

the previous two months, he doubted their ability to survive a night stranded 4,000 feet up a mountain. Later, he described what followed as a return to "youthful days". Worsley was rather more forthcoming: "I straddled behind Sir Ernest, holding his shoulder. Crean did the same to me, and so, locked together, we let go." They shot off down the slope and into the darkness. "I was never more scared in my life for the first 30 seconds," Worsley admitted. The human toboggan plummeted down the mountainside before crashing into a bank of soft snow. "We stood up and shook hands – very pleased with ourselves." They had descended 3,000 feet in two minutes.

Shunning sleep, the three men continued marching towards Stromness, and at six-thirty the next morning, Shackleton heard the steam whistle that roused the whalers from their beds. By lunchtime, they were gazing down upon a ship moored in the bay, and a few hours later they entered the whaling station. The first people they encountered were two young boys. The pair stopped in their tracks and stared open-mouthed at the three dishevelled creatures, who, with their

unkempt hair, shambolic beards and shredded clothes, had a wild look about them. The boys ran screaming for their fathers.

The explorers found the station manager's house and introduced themselves. Shackleton told their story, then asked if it would be possible for the three of them to have a bath and a razor: "Within an hour or two we had ceased to be savages and had become civilized men again."

Elephant Island

On April 25, the day after the *James Caird* had sailed from Elephant Island, Frank Wild gathered the remaining 21 men around him and issued a rallying call. There would be no slacking over the coming weeks as they awaited a rescue that, he assured them, would come.

The first problem facing the men was how to build a shelter that would protect them from the

Home sweet home: the living quarters for the 22 men left on Elephant Island.

gales and blizzards that battered their camp. They were perched precariously on a spit that jutted into the sea and was less than 100 feet across. A more exposed spot would be difficult to imagine. "Life here without a hut and equipment is about beyond endurance," wrote Frank Hurley, the tough Australian photographer.

After an attempt to carve an ice cave in the glacier proved unsuccessful, Wild ordered their two boats to be turned turtle and placed on top of two walls constructed of boulders. Strips of canvas torn from some of the tents (which had proved wholly inadequate against the 90mph winds) were draped over the boats to seal any openings against the blizzards. It was a primitive home, but one that stood up to even the sternest of tests. Not long after the men moved into their new accommodation, a hurricane swept in: "Each gust heralds its approach by a low rumbling which increases to a thunderous roar. Snow, stones and gravel are flying about, and any gear left unweighted by very heavy stones is carried away to sea."

Despite the weather, the men went out each day in search of penguins and seals, and a copious supply kept the cook busy for much of the day. At least the glaciers provided a limitless supply of drinking water. The one drawback of the cook's activity was black blubber soot, which pervaded every nook and cranny of the men's clothing and formed a thick layer on the inside of the boats, getting into their eyes and throats.

When the men weren't out hunting, they passed the time of day by reading books, sewing or, most commonly, talking about food. They planned imaginary banquets and discussed the food they would demand first when they returned to England. "Any old dumpling," said Wild, "so long as it was a large one." Wild proved a tower of strength throughout the weeks they spent on Elephant Island. "A magnificent leader," said Alexander Macklin, "popular and respected by everyone."

Macklin himself earned the respect of the men when he and the other surgeon, James McIlroy, carried out an operation on Percy Blackborrow's left foot. All five toes had become frostbitten during the journey from the floe to Elephant Island, and the two surgeons were concerned that gangrene would set in if they didn't amputate them. One morning, after constructing an operating table from old nut boxes, the pair removed Blackborrow's toes in an operation that lasted less than an hour.

During all the weeks spent wedged under the upturned hulls of the two boats, Wild never tolerated any talk among the men about the fate of the *James Caird*. He had total faith in Shackleton and each morning would rouse the men by telling them to look sharp, because that day could be the day Shackleton appeared with a ship. But when July turned into August and there was still no sign of salvation, some of the men began to voice their concern. On August 28, 126 days since waving goodbye to the *James Caird*, one of the men wrote in his diary, "I will give them until about September 10th and after that I shall think that something has happened to them."

Rescue

Having bathed, shaved and enjoyed his first proper meal for 18 months, Shackleton turned his attention to the rescue of the remaining 25 men. His immediate priority was to pick up the three left behind with the *James Caird* in King Haakon Bay, and a few hours after arriving in Stromness, Worsley was on his way in a whaler to collect them. Meanwhile, Shackleton rushed around the station, desperate to secure a vessel to take him to Elephant Island as soon as possible.

When Worsley returned with McNeish,

Bloodied but unbowed the men on Elephant Island refused to give up hope of rescue.

McCarthy and Vincent, Shackleton arranged their passage back to England while he, Crean and Worsley prepared to depart for Elephant Island. They had been given the use of a steam whaler called *Southern Sky*, and they sailed from South Georgia on May 23.

Three days later, Shackleton was becoming increasingly worried by the drop in temperature and the thin film of ice that lay on the sea. Conditions worsened steadily until, on May 28, the pack ice forced them back, only 70 miles from Elephant Island. "To admit failure at this stage was hard," he wrote, "but the facts had to be faced."

Next, Shackleton sought help from South America, the Uruguayan Government lending him a trawler called *Institutio Pesca, No.1*. She arrived at the Falkland Islands (where the *Southern Sky* had dropped Shackleton and his two companions) on June 16. As she sailed into Port Stanley, her appearance didn't inspire Shackleton with much confidence, but the vessel managed to get within 20 miles of Elephant Island before, once again, the pack ice prevented further progress.

Eventually, the Chilean Government stepped into the breach, after much begging on Shackleton's part, and loaned him a steamer called *Yelco*, on the understanding that she was not to be risked in the pack ice. Shackleton happily agreed to this condition, as word had reached him that the end of the southern winter had seen off the last of the ice, and it was open sea all the way.

On the evening of August 29, the ship was 60

Ship Ahoy! The Yelco steams into view and the waiting is finally over.

miles from the island. On the next morning, Shackleton awoke to find a curtain of fog in front of them. A couple of hours later, however, the curtain parted and there, dead ahead, were the menacing cliffs of Elephant Island.

Wild was just beginning to serve lunch under one of the boats, when George Marston came tearing along the beach and dived through the entrance. "There's a ship!" he screamed. "There's a ship!" Chaos ensued as the men scrambled outside to see this miracle for themselves. As they tumbled out from beneath the boat, Shackleton counted them through his binoculars. "I heard his strained tones as he counted the figures," remembered Worsley. "'Two-five-seven,' and then an exultant shout, 'They're all there, Skipper. They are all safe!' His face lit up and years seemed to fall off his age."

Shackleton and Crean went ashore in a boat as the men dashed up and down the beach like excited schoolchildren. "I felt jolly near blubbing," confessed Wild. A packet of cigarettes was tossed from the boat, and the men fell on them like hungry tigers. Fearful that a change of wind would usher back the ice at any moment, Shackleton wasted no time in getting the men on board the *Yelco*, where food and drink awaited them. "We got the men on board at 1pm," recalled Worsley, "and by 1am there was not a drop of liqueur left."

The return to war

From the time the *Endurance* was abandoned to the moment the *Yelco* arrived at Elephant Island, two topics dominated the conversation. The first was food, and the second was the war. The men spent many an hour, sheltering in a tent or under a boat, discussing the war they had left behind all those months before. When Shackleton, Crean and Worsley arrived at Stromness whaling station, one of the first questions they asked the manager was, "When was the war over?" Shackleton

remembered how the manager had looked at them and replied, "The war is not over. Millions are being killed. Europe is mad. The world is mad."

When he sailed in the *Yelco*, Shackleton had taken with him a collection of old newspapers for the men to read. An air of stunned disbelief pervaded the ship as they digested the news of wholesale slaughter on land and sea. By the beginning of October, 1916, nearly all the men were sailing back to England, eager to join the fight against Germany. "The same energy and endurance that they showed in the Antarctic they brought to the greater war in the Old World," wrote Shackleton in *South*.

By the time that the war ended, in 1918, two of the men from the *Endurance* expedition had been killed in the fighting. One of them was Tim McCarthy, who went down with his ship three weeks after landing in England. It seemed so unfair to Shackleton that McCarthy had survived an 800-mile voyage in a 22-foot boat across treacherous seas, only to drown a few months later.

Even at the height of the First World War, the story of *Endurance* made headlines around the world. It was a welcome distraction for the British public and newspapers in a year when the war had not gone well. As with Scott in 1912, the papers glossed over the fact that the expedition had been a failure. No one from the *Endurance* had even set foot on Antarctica, and Shackleton's claim that "important scientific work had been carried out" was spurious to say the least. But the story of the men's survival against overwhelming odds, and their refusal to give up hope, struck a chord with the British people. Shackleton was hailed as a symbol of courage and determination. He was the morale booster that the nation needed.

Shackleton attributed his own survival to something more than courage and determination. He was not a religious man, but when he reflected on the expedition, he had little doubt that providence had looked after them. Worsley felt the same, and years later, when his mind drifted back to the crossing of the South Georgian mountains, he would find himself counting the party: "Shackleton, Crean, and I and – who was the other? Of course, they were only three...but I had a curious feeling on the march that there was another person with us."

But to suggest that the expedition's survival relied purely on providence is modesty on Shackleton's part. His firm and confident leadership, his courage, his loyalty to his men, and his refusal to admit defeat pulled them through. He inspired and cajoled his men through moments of enormous terror and great suffering. A hint of doubt from Shackleton could have caused panic among the men, but not once did he waver. "Being a born leader," Worsley wrote of Shackleton, "he had to lead in the positions of most danger, difficulty and responsibility. I have seen him turn pale, yet force himself into the post of greatest peril. That was his type of courage; he would do the job that he was most afraid of."

Heroes of the Antarctic

Sir Ernest Shackleton

Having been commissioned into the Army as a major, Shackleton embarked on a series of lectures after the war, but by early 1920 he had become ill and was drinking too much. A former school friend came to the rescue and offered to fund another expedition south. Shackleton jumped at the chance and sailed from England in the *Quest* in September, 1921. On board were several members from the *Endurance* expedition.

Shackleton's grave on South Georgia (above) and aboard Quest *in 1921.*

On January 4, 1922, the *Quest* arrived in South Georgia, and Shackleton became happy again. "A wonderful evening," he wrote in his diary that night. However, at shortly before 3am on the morning of the fifth, he died from a massive heart attack. He was 47. His men transported the body to Uruguay, with the intention of returning their leader to England, but Emily cabled them and told them to lay her husband to rest in South Georgia. She knew that this was what he would have wanted.

Frank Wild

Wild took command of the *Quest* expedition, but without Shackleton, he lost much of the drive and purpose that had proved so invaluable on previous expeditions. The *Quest* returned to England in June, 1922, after Wild had sailed her to Elephant Island to catch a final glimpse of the camp where he had survived for four months in

1916. Later, he emigrated to South Africa and became a cotton farmer, but drought destroyed his business and he found solace in alcohol while working in a public house. He died, destitute, in 1939, aged 65.

Frank Worsley

Worsley was also on the *Quest* expedition, having joined Shackleton from Russia, where he had been awarded a second Distinguished Service Order (DSO) for bravery while fighting the Bolsheviks. He had won his first DSO during the First World War when, as commander of a destroyer, he had sunk a German submarine. He became joint leader of the British Arctic Expedition in 1925, and for many of the subsequent 15 years, he sailed the world, seeking – and finding – adventure. On the outbreak of the Second World War, Worsley tried to join the Merchant Navy, but his age prevented him from taking command of a ship. He died of cancer in 1943, aged 70.

Tom Crean

After years of hair-raising adventures in Antarctica – he was awarded the Albert Medal for saving Teddy Evans's life in 1912 – the unflappable Tom Crean slipped quietly back into civilian life after serving in the Navy during the First World War. He opened a public house in his native County Kerry, called *The South Pole Inn*, married and rarely strayed far from his home and his dogs. He died in 1938, aged 62, one of the unsung heroes of Antarctica.

Roald Amundsen

In 1914, Amundsen learned to fly, and 11 years later, he made the furthest journey north in an aeroplane. In the following year, he made the first flight over the Arctic in an airship called *Norge*, crossing from Spitsbergen to Alaska in two days. In 1927, he published his memoirs, *My Life as an Explorer*, but he was becoming increasingly bored and disillusioned with life. A year later, by then aged 55, Amundsen was asked to help search the Arctic for an Italian explorer who had vanished. He took off from Tromso in Norway on June 18, 1928, and was never seen again.

Roald Amundsen's mysterious death was in some ways a fitting end for such an enigmatic man.

Apsley Cherry-Garrard

Cherry-Garrard never fully recovered from his experiences in Antarctica, being described in later years by a colleague from the expedition as "overthrown and disordered by dwelling on a far-off past of glorious friendship and perhaps a needlessly uneasy conscience about the part he played".

Cherry-Garrard commanded a squadron of armoured cars during the First World War, but he was invalided back to England, where he wrote *The Worst Journey In The World*. This was published in 1922 to huge acclaim. The remainder of his life was spent quietly on his 300-acre estate, where he took a keen interest in exploration. He married in 1939 and, at last, began to find some peace of mind as he and his wife travelled extensively throughout Europe. Gradually, however, his health deteriorated, and he died in 1959, aged 73.

Tom Crean (left) lived out his days in Ireland and died peacefully in 1938.

Bibliography

Scott & Amundsen: The Race to the South Pole, Roland Huntford.

Scott's Men, David Thompson.

North Pole, South Pole: Journeys to the Ends of the Earth, Bertrand Imbert.

Polar Exploration, Terence Wise.

The Endurance, Caroline Alexander.

Edward Wilson of the Antarctic, George Seaver.

A First-Rate Tragedy, Diana Preston.

Captain Oates, Sue Limb and Patrick Cordingley.

Nothing Venture, Nothing Win, Sir Edmund Hillary.

Shackleton, Roland Huntford.

Shackleton's Boat Journey, F.A. Worsley.

South, Sir Ernest Shackleton.

Scott of the Antarctic, George Seaver.

Scott of the Antarctic, Elspeth Huxley.

The Worst Journey In The World, Apsley Cherry-Garrard.

Scott's memorial cross on Observation Hill, Antarctica.

Index

PICTURE CREDITS

The publishers would like to thank the following sources for their kind permission to reproduce the pictures in this book:

Corbis 17, 32, 54, 83, 110, 111/The Academy of Natural Sciences of Philadelphia 35, 46, 47/Bettmann 58, 125r/Hulton-Deutsch Collection 14, 15, 21r, 40r, 54bl, 59/Peter Johnson 24b/Wolfgang Kaehler 44, 88, 124tl/Kit Kittle 8tr/Graham Neden; Ecoscene 50/PEMCO - Webster & Stevens Collection 56/Galen Rowell 10, 11/Underwood & Underwood 31, 100, 104, 105
Mary Evans Picture Library 13, 23t, 39, 48, 51cr, 79
Hulton Getty 10tl, 12br, 16, 18, 19, 21l, 22, 25, 26tl, 27, 30, 36, 40l, 49b, 51, 57, 65, 71, 72, 80, 85, 86, 90bc, 92, 94, 102, 122, 124b
Image Bank 101
Landscape map of Antarctica from Phillip's Modern Atlas School 6
Popperfoto 5bl, 5tl, 20, 28, 29, 33, 34, 37, 49t, 52, 60, 61, 62, 64, 66, 68, 70, 73, 74, 75, 76, 77, 81, 83, 96, 102t
Royal Geographical Society, London 91, 97, 98, 106, 107, 108, 112, 114, 118, 120, 125bl
Science Photo Library 23b
Scott Polar Research Institute 26, 41, 116
Tony Stone Images 1, 2, 3, 4, 9, 38
Topham 5, 126